V

THE TAO OF
MUHAMMAD ALI·

Davis Miller

THE TAO OF MUHAMMAD ALI

VINTAGE

Published by Vintage 1997

10 9

Copyright © Davis Worth Miller 1996

The right of Davis Worth Miller to be identified as the author
of this work has been asserted by him in accordance
with the Copyright, Designs and Patents Act, 1988.

Portions of this story have appeared in various forms in *Esquire*, *Sports Illustrated*, *Men's
Journal*, *Sport* magazine, *Legends* magazine, *Playboy* (Japanese edition), *Penthouse* (South
African edition) and *Karate International*; and in magazines published by the Louisville
Courier-Journal, the Miami *Herald*, the Chicago *Tribune*, the Cleveland *Plain Dealer*, the
Pittsburgh *Post-Gazette*, the Detroit *Free Press*, the Dallas *Morning News*, the Buffalo *News*,
the Washington *Post* and the Denver *Post*, as well as in feature sections of the Louisville
Courier-Journal, the Washington *Post*, the Houston *Chronicle*, the Seattle *Times*, the
Winston-Salem *Journal*, the Toledo *Blade*, the Grand Rapids *Press*, the South Ireland
Independent, and *Folha de São Paolo* (Brazil); and in sports sections of the Los Angeles *Times*,
the Indianapolis *Star*, the Winston-Salem *Journal* and the Louisville *Courier Journal*.
Portions of Chapters Twenty-two, Twenty-six, Twenty-eight, Twenty-nine and Thirty-six
appeared in different forms as 'The Zen of Muhammad Ali' in *The Best American Sports
Writing of 1994*.

Thanks to the editors at all of the magazines and newspapers who, although this didn't fit
the format of their periodicals, trusted the writing and the story

This book was completed with a Creative Nonfiction Writers' Project Grant from
the North Carolina Arts Council

First published in the United States of America by
Warner Books, Inc., 1996

Vintage
Random House, 20 Vauxhall Bridge Road, London SW1V 2SA

addresses for companies within The Random House Group Limited
can be found at:
www.randomhouse.co.uk/offices.htm

The Random House Group Limited Reg. No. 954009
www.randomhouse.co.uk

A CIP catalogue record for this book
is available from the British Library

ISBN 9780099753414

The Random House Group Limited supports The Forest Stewardship
Council (FSC®), the leading international forest certification organisation.
Our books carrying the FSC label are printed on FSC® certified paper. FSC is
the only forest certification scheme endorsed by the leading environmental
organisations, including Greenpeace. Our paper procurement policy can be
found at www.randomhouse.co.uk/environment

Printed and bound by
CPI Group (UK) Ltd, Croydon, CR0 4YY

A VINTAGE ORIGINAL

To Roy L. Miller,
the best father I could ever imagine having had.

And for Lynn.

Sincere admiration and immeasurable thanks to my newly adopted grandfather (and the godfather of this book), Armand S. Deutsch.

A special tap of the mitts to Terry. This book is as much yours as mine, old friend.

The Greatest Thank Yous of All Times to Cam Benty, Stephen Brunt, Denis Gosselin, Holly Haverty, Greg Johnson, Bill Linthicum, Kathy Long, Debbie McGill, Dave McGinty, Craig Mortali, Eric Nolan, Laura Shepherd, Tom Shroder, Tom Simons, Terri Smith, George Tan, Beth Thomas, Gene Weingarten, and Greg Williams for friendship, (numerous) readings, editing, schooling, and advice; to Len Irish for the great photos and to Howard for making them happen. Thanks also to Mel Berger, Norman Brokaw, and Peter Nelson for respect, attentiveness, and for helping me make my mortgage payments.

A ring center bow to my editor, Rick Wolff, for allowing me to write the best story I had in me.

Thanks to Maya Angelou, for helping me see that there are no shortcuts to writing with wisdom.

To Lonnie, for being a gentle listener and for being Muhammad's angel.

And of course to Muhammad, for bringing me to my best self—and to Gail for continually reminding me who that self is (and is not).

Contents

Author's Note

———————————

We struggle. Always.
We are doing the best that we can.
And we dream of transcendence.
For me, there was a time when the dream was incarnate.

And the dream's name was Muhammad Ali.

This is the story of my time spent with that dream.
Although the narrative is not always historically accurate, and although some chronology and numerous details have been changed for dramatic effect, it is, in essence, true.

"... In movement, how like a god."

William Shakespeare, *Hamlet*

"The atmosphere of our planet circulates so regularly and efficiently that every breath we take contains molecules expulsed by Siddhartha Gautama."

Robert Ripley

"Though much is taken, much abides; and though
We are not now that strength which in old days
Moved earth and heaven, that which we are, we
are."

Alfred, Lord Tennyson, *Ulysses*

"In every act of destruction
there is an act of creation."

Albert Einstein

"The superior man
when he has found success in the world
abandons it and moves to the country."

Lao Tzu

Prologue

I first met him atop his Pennsylvania mountain in July 1975, though I had seen him thousands of times.

While pulling on a pair of blood-red Everlast trunks I'd bought just for this occasion, I heard him through the dressing-room walls, exhorting the small crowd of spectators who had paid one dollar each to watch him train. "I will prove to the whole world that I am not only the greatest boxer of all times," he said, "I am the greatest martial artist."

Even through the walls, his was the most elemental voice I'd heard; it was huge, melodic, and sounded somehow eternal. Listening to him made me so nervous that I shook a little and felt that I needed to pee. The old guy standing in front of me, strapping a pair of rich-smelling red leather gloves on my arms, looked at me and laughed. "He won't hurt a little white boy like you," he said.

I was twenty-two years old, hard-bodied as a bee, and I no longer thought of myself as "little" or a "white boy." The old guy was stooped; his eyes were yellow with age. His long, serious face was hard and soft. There was street life all over his features, but also a gentleness. "Naw, he won't hurt you," he told me again. "Not too bad anyways."

When he finished tying the gloves, he taped the laces down, and left the room, I paced back and forth, staring at the reptilian-barked logs in the walls. When I couldn't stand the wait any longer, I walked out the back door and stepped barefoot past the boulders that had been placed in a circle around the cabin. On each rock, a name had been painted in bold red- and blue-trimmed white block letters. I read the names: Willie Pep and Ray Robinson, Jack Dempsey and Gene Tunney, Rocky Marciano and Archie Moore, Sonny Liston and Joe Frazier. A rounded chunk of brown lichen-covered granite called Joe Louis had been granted the most honored position, in front of the main entrance to the gym. I listened to a freight train moaning somewhere a long way off. I watched the mailman come and go. "Good luck, son," he said, giggling.

I walked back around the side of the cabin and climbed the biggest boulder of all, a flat-topped, five-foot-high hunk of hard black coal named Jack Johnson. I stood on the rock, gloved hands at my sides. To calm myself and get my lungs started, I shut my eyes and drew four deep slow breaths. I'd never known my body as well as I did then. I swear I could feel oxygen rush all the way to my toes with each breath I took. With closed eyes, I imagined the very power of the cosmos flowing up from the boulder and into my torso.

Today, there will be no more talk about size. I feel myself growing in every instant. I've been patient, so patient, waiting for this for so long. I feel old skin fall away. I step from it, shining.

I turn my back to the cabin and snort the air, smelling the sweet smells of ironweed, clover, and horse sweat. I stare past the buckboard and stables, down the steep hill, at coin-bright leaves on beeches and poplars, on sugar maples and oaks, and I let their richness fill my head until all I see is green.

He's standing in the center of his ring when I part the ropes and step through. Insect-looking splotches of dried blood dot the porous canvas under my feet. As I stare up at him, he comes into focus and everything else blurs. And I realize once again that no one else on the planet looks quite like him. His skin is unmarked and without wrinkles, and he glows in a way that cannot be seen in photographs or on television.

He introduces me to the crowd as a "great karate master," an accolade I certainly don't merit. Then he opens his mouth wide, points his gloved left fist at me, and in a voice directed to no one in particular but to the world in general, he shouts, "You must be a fool to get in the ring with me. When I'm through, you gowna think you been whupped by Bruce Lee.

"Are you scared?" he asks, looking at me straight and level. "Are you scared? Just think who you're with. How's it feel, knowin' you're in the ring with the Greatest of All Times?"

He turns from me and back to the crowd. "I am the center of the universe," he proclaims, and I almost believe him.

The bell rings and he dances to my right around the twenty-foot square of taut canvas. Suddenly I'm no longer nervous. My thighs are strong and springy, there's looseness in my movement. The fine layer of sweat on my skin feels like something intrinsic and unnameable that has to come out.

He bounces from side to side in front of me; I feel every step he takes shoot into my feet and up my legs. I bend to the right, toss a jab toward his belt line, straighten up, snap a long, tentative front kick to his head. I figure it's the first kick he's ever had thrown at him, but he pulls away as easily as if he's been dodging feet his entire life. He stops dancing and stands flat-footed in front of me, studying my movements. God, what a big man. I try to lever in a jab from the outside, where it's usually easiest for me to connect. His eyes are snappingly bright. His face is beaming and round and open. He waits until my punch is about a half inch from his nose and he pulls his head straight back. I punch nothing but air and dreams. He turns square toward me, teases me by sticking out a long, white-coated tongue, steps back to the ropes, takes a seat on the second strand, where his head is just about level with mine, and beckons me in with a wave of his gloves.

I block out spectators' laughs and slide inside his arms three half steps; he's so close I feel his breath on my shoulder. I dig a roundkick into his right kidney, feel his flesh conform to the shape of my shin, see the opening I'm hoping for, fake a jab, and explode from my crouch, rocketing a spinning backfist–left hook combination straight into the center of the right side of his jaw. As the punches connect, they feel so good that I smile. People in the crowd ooh and aah.

He opens his eyes fried-egg wide in feigned disbelief. He has never thought of me before, will never think of me as a fighter again, but for two seconds I deserve his serious attention. For two long seconds we are inseparably bound, whirling in a circle of electricity, each seeing nothing but the other. For two week-long seconds I am flying. Then he squashes me with just one flyswatter jab.

I see the punch coming; it's a piece of red cinnamon candy exactly the size of a gloved fist. I try to move away and can't—it's that fast. The back of my head bounces off of my shoulders. A chorus of white light goes off behind my eyes. There's a metal taste in my mouth, then a second, heavier thump. The spectators suddenly sound way, way off; my legs go to soup beneath me.

He knows I'm hurt and he steps back. It's obvious he could knock me out with a single punch. I'm sure that most boxers would be pleased to do so. Instead, his eyes go kind, he slides an arm around my shoulders, we exchange hugs and smiles, and it's over.

But I've accomplished something I've never, yet always, believed I'd have the opportunity to do.

I have boxed with Muhammad Ali.

As we leave the ring together, the greatest of all pugilists speaks in a way few men have ever spoken to me—softly, gently, almost purring. "You're fast," he says. "And you sure can hit, to be *sssooo* little."

He may as well have said he was adopting me.

I begin to quake. My insides dance. But I manage to stay composed long enough to say the one thing I hope will (and that seems to) impress him most. With the absolute confidence I've learned from watching him on television and hearing him on the radio countless times, I say simply, "I know."

SECTION I

An Initiation

One

Some people study faults in the earth's crust or the habits of storms or of galaxies, hoping to make sense of the universe and of their own lives. Others meditate on the life and work of one social movement or one man. For you to understand all that Muhammad Ali has meant to me, I need to show you where I came from; I must tell you a few of my secrets.

But let me warn you: Once the telling starts, there's no beginning and no end to the stories, this bevy of elephants connected to one another, laced trunks to tails.

The first time I saw Ali was in late January 1964. I had just turned twelve and was the shortest and skinniest and sickliest kid in town. My mother had died unexpectedly only a few months before.

I scarcely remember any event that took place before my mother's death. And I suppose I have few real memories of her and the time before she died because, after she did, I no longer wanted to remember.

My mother. I hardly recall what she looked like. I remember that she had long, curly blond hair and a smallish mouth that, like mine, revealed her moods in the ways that it moved. I remember that when she took naps she rocked herself to sleep by moving gently from side to side. Most of what I know, though, I see from the photograph I'm holding in front of me now. Daddy told me that it was taken in October 1947. She was seventeen, it was her senior year in high school, and the picture was snapped the day after she was elected homecoming queen of Hanes High in Winston-Salem, North Carolina.

The girl I see in the picture is seated in a white wicker chair. Her small ivory hands are folded in her lap and she's holding a single red rose. Although the situation is formal, her facial expression doesn't look posed. She has deep-set, slightly foreboding eyes, is thin, pale, fragile, and pretty. In less than a year, she was to be married to the boy who had been her steady sweetheart since she was five years old. Daddy used to tell my sister and me, "She's one of those people who was a little too gentle for this world."

I remember the small capped bottles of my mother's urine that seemed always to be stored behind the apples and pears and summer squash in the back of the refrigerator on the bottom shelf. I recall that in late July 1963, my father and mother and sister and I left our house in a brand-new Chevrolet Impala (the first new car Daddy had been able to afford), bound for Florida and our first-ever two-week vacation. Five days later, all four of us were on a central Florida highway; Daddy was driving home as fast as he could. My mother was running a fever of 105; she was sweating and delirious. We had to pull off the road every few miles for her to vomit in the roadside weeds. The following afternoon, back in Winston-Salem, I recall being bored and wanting to leave the room when she asked me to sit on her bed and read her my Donald Duck comic book just before the ambulance came. My mother died that evening at age thirty-two of a rare kidney disease that could be diagnosed only during autopsy.

Four years before her death, when I was seven, my father and mother bought an acre of what had once been pasture and built a house there between a dirt road and a rolling, rambling creek. Winston-Salem is located in the Appalachian foothills and our acre was bordered on both the east and west by steep inclines and what was left of the area's ancient pine and cedar forests—forests whose rising, glowing morning mists, tinted by pigments in the needles, give the Blue Ridge Mountains their name.

I spent a lot of time by myself down by the creek and up among big oaks and sycamores to the east, playing in great green ghostlike formations of kudzu that dominated the woods. I'd swing from the kudzu's

itchy vines and tromp through its waist-deep meadows. I'd dig up old green cow bones from under the
vines, mostly thighs and shoulders and ribs, although
I'd find an occasional skull. I'd bring them home and
place them on a stump in the backyard until Daddy
came in from work and made me go throw them in
the creek so they wouldn't upset my mother.

My mother. This story is not about her, but her
ghost hides somewhere on every page. Because I was
in my early twenties before I quit blaming myself for
her death.

The reasons that I blamed myself were ambiguous.
Aunts and uncles had told me that my mother's doctor advised her not to have children. But she had me
and then my sister. I thought that Carol and I may
have made her die.

For a couple of years before my mother's death,
many nights I'd lie in bed and listen to my parents
yell at each other about money and about my father's
best friend, who often called my mother while Daddy
was at work. I'd sometimes hear Daddy slam the back
door, start the car, and drive away. As I lay sleepless,
waiting for him to come home, I thought that my
parents might get divorced. I prayed through most of
each night and day in early 1963 that they would not.
I saw my mother's death as the unambiguous answer
to that prayer.

It wasn't long after she died that I lost a lot of
weight. I no longer wanted to eat or even to drink. I
eventually spent a couple of weeks in the hospital,
where I was pumped full of glucose and fluids be-

cause I'd become dehydrated. When I got out of the hospital, every day as I walked to school I counted each step I took. And as I walked and counted, I prayed. "Dear God," I said, sometimes aloud and sometimes to myself, "bless Mommy and Daddy and Carol and Jet and Tippy and Uncle Tom and Aunt Lib and please, please, please, God, please keep Daddy safe and healthy all day long."

Although I'd previously excelled in my studies, I lost interest in what went on in the classroom. "Davis is always daydreaming," Mrs. McClure, my fifth-grade teacher, wrote on my report card.

What Mrs. McClure didn't know is that I thought of the houseflies that landed on my desk as angels. I talked to the flies, asked them how my mother was. The angels did not answer.

I left books at school, threw them in the mud. When Daddy asked if I had homework, I told him that I'd already done it or that none had been assigned. I had few friends, and the ones I had were boys. I quit talking to girls. Although I was attracted to them, I was scared that if I allowed myself to get close to one, she'd soon leave me.

Just before the Thanksgiving holiday, Mrs. McClure assigned a paper to write in class called "Looking Out the Window."

"Outside my window," I wrote, "it is pitch black dark. I don't see a thing."

Then, about four months after my mother's death, I began my second life, the secret one that was seeded by the heroes in twelve-cent comic books:

Superman, the Flash, the Mighty Thor, the Green Lantern. Invulnerable heroes blessed with powers they knew they had to hide from the ordinary people around them. Heroes who always wanted women but who never touched them, forsaking personal pleasure and happiness in order to crusade against the forces of evil. I bought every comic I could get my hands on.

Especially Superman. The Man of Tomorrow. The guy with the greatest powers and long, lean musculature; his body not hypertrophic, as were those of some of the other superheroes. The original after whom everybody else had been patterned. Even Superman's outfit was the classic of the genre: bold red cape and boots and insignia highlighted by a vibrant yellow trim against a bright blue field. The blue the color of the sky in March and April. Oh, to be a creature of sky: to fly, to be free. If only I could.

When I wasn't at school or reading comics, I spent nearly every waking moment staring miserably at the television. I talked occasionally to my father and less to my sister, but I was mostly silent. Much of the time I was content to watch free movies that rolled behind my eyes. They were fanciful adventures I saw, talismanic action stories I crafted. In them I was strong and straight and right and brave. All women longed for me. All men looked down when in my presence. I was everything expected of me by everyone. I could bounce from telephone pole to telephone pole, run across golden plains with impalas, swim through sunlight-dappled water with dolphins, lift houses from their foundations, conquer all assailants with beautiful, well-placed blows.

This was the period during which I first saw Ali (the black Superman), when he was still Cassius Clay. Clay had recently turned twenty-two, and heat rose shimmering around his sleek, hard body as he prepared to meet Sonny Liston for the world heavyweight championship. I remember sitting mesmerized in front of Daddy's small black-and-white television as Clay's voice roared and crackled from the huge world outside and through the TV's rattling three-inch speaker. "I'm young and handsome and fast and pretty and can't possibly be beat," the voice announced. The song the voice sang roiled with menace and grace. And, although I couldn't have said it, for me the voice was cooking with the cosmic.

Since then, many of the events that have defined my life have been related to Ali.

At seventeen, I was the smallest kid at R. J. Reynolds High School in Winston-Salem: I was four-foot-ten, weighed sixty-three pounds, and looked maybe eleven years old. The family doctor told Daddy that I'd never get much larger. Guys in my classes nicknamed me "Fetus." I was regularly punched in the stomach, pushed into girls' restrooms, shoved fully clothed into showers, stuffed into lockers, picked up over guys' heads and spun in circles until they put me on the ground and my hair was standing on end while the rest of me was lying down.

I still had no interest in school. I had failed Spanish I three times, P.E. twice, and freshman, sophomore, and junior English once each. I flunked the eleventh grade and would not be able to graduate until I was at least nineteen. Three to four times every month, I was caught skipping school. Usually, when I cut class, I didn't have anyplace to go and I stayed in the building, creeping down the halls from one bathroom to the next (the best way to avoid getting caught was to spend as much time as possible in the john), combing my hair in the mirrors above the sinks. When I attended class, I laid my head on my desk and slept.

But I had Ali.

And the music in his voice that seemed to roll up in great hopeful waves from deep in his abdomen.

Throughout the sixties, I followed Ali in his victories over numerous lesser mortals. Part of the obvious appeal of watching Ali in the ring was the perceived fragility about him, the sense that to be this beautiful he must be in mortal danger all the time. Ali himself, Ali the cosmic brat, cultured this view. Could any warrior ever have looked so vulnerable as the young Ali—with his shining and tender chin high and untucked, angular poet's body fully erect, hands at his sides, eyes round and wide and scared-seeming virtually every moment he was in the ring—even as he shocked opponents and blistered their features with a (burning) bushel of punches thrown from angles and with a rapidity that they, and we, could scarcely conceive of, much less see?

In his bout with Brian London, at the beginning of Round Three, in just two seconds' time—one Mississippi, two Mississippi—Ali launched and landed a mind-numbing series of seventeen punches. London bowed, he fell, he lay, sprawled on the canvas. The reason it took London a full two seconds to fall is that Ali's punches had come in such volume that they had held London up. When Ali quit throwing, he stepped back and thrust his arms, godlike, above his head. Ali's (proven) thesis was this: The "prettiest" is also the most efficient. What greater defense could there be for art?

Sitting in front of Daddy's television, I shook my head from side to side. How could anyone, much less a man as huge as Ali, a six-three giant who weighed 210, snap out better than eight concussive punches in a single second? Not to mention that all the blows had struck a moving target. Yet I had seen Ali do it. At least I had seen the tracers his gloves left in passing.

I bought a copy of the Ali biography by Jose Torres, *Sting Like a Bee*. In it I discovered that my birthday was two days before Ali's—his was January 17, mine the fifteenth—and that his wife Belinda studied karate under an instructor named George Dillman. I began taking *kyokushinkai* karate because there was no boxing in town and I longed to become as fine a fistic artist as Ali. I bought a *gi* (Japanese for "uniform"), attended class religiously, and worked as hard as a sixty-three-pound runt could—I kicked at the walls, punched the air countless hundreds of times, sweat and hurt under the fluorescent lights for an hour and a half four nights a week. After a year and a half of study, I was awarded a brown belt, the second-highest belt rank. I read everything I could about the martial arts and about boxing and, of course, about Ali. In addition to practicing kyokushinkai, I stood before the full-length mirror in the hall, pushing my worm of a left arm out at the reflection, trying feebly to imitate Ali's cobra jab.

All the exercise stimulated both my appetite and my confidence; I gained about five pounds, which, in turn, made me feel still better about myself. I inched out of my shell and began talking some, even cracking an occasional joke. And I began to take pride in my appearance. Some girls took interest, but I was still scared of them. "Kid Karate" and "Billy Jack," the girls called me in my junior yearbook.

Hey, Bird Fetus, you going to the Feti convention at the graveyard this weekend? Ha, Ha.

Watts

Davis,
Why are all the boys so mean to you? You're really not a bad guy. And your karate moves are so cute. See ya this fall.

Love ya,
Debbie

Fetis,
I'll tell you why. You sux more than any little s.o.b.
that I have every run across in my life. Why don't
you try your dam best to get out of RJR before your
hair turns gray. You could take karate for ten years
and you might be able to beat your meat. I guess I'll
see you this summer at the Tavern if your not to
drunk off 2 talls.

Shore

Daddy enrolled me in Miss Winnie Cederick's School of Dance Arts, hoping, he later told me, that an introductory ballroom course would help bring me out still more.

Winnie Cederick had been a Radio City Rockette. In Winston-Salem, this was enough to allow her a kind of fame. If Miss Cederick had ever been girlish, there was little about her to indicate it. Daddy called Miss Cederick a striking woman, which was his kind way of saying that he found her less than attractive. She was tall, wore her steel garbage-can-colored hair piled high in a beehive, and chain-smoked Lucky Strikes while she taught.

The ballroom classes at Miss Cederick's were at three-thirty on Wednesdays. The first couple of lessons went fine. I even sort of enjoyed myself and was looking forward to the third, when Miss Cederick was supposed to pair us off for the first time. For the first time in my life, I'd get to dance with a real live girl. That Wednesday morning, I wore my Sunday best to school and between classes I went to the bathroom to comb my hair.

When school was over, I had four blocks to walk to Miss Cederick's and only fifteen minutes before the lesson started; I'd need to rush. On the way out the door, I stopped to check my hair and to tuck my shirt in my pants. I needed to pee, but didn't think I had time. I ran all the way to Miss Cederick's and burst through the door right as my name was being called.

"Davis Miller," Miss Cederick announced, biting down hard on her cigarette. My name echoed across the polished wood dance floor. "And Cindi Dollar," she continued.

My mouth dropped open like the business end of a dump truck. Cindi Dollar, the finest-looking cheerleader in the whole school, and probably the entire western hemisphere. Every guy had the hots for Cindi. Not only was she beautiful, she was rich. Her dad was a vice president at R. J. Reynolds Tobacco Company. I stared at Cindi from across the floor. Her shining blond hair flowed down her shoulders and disappeared behind her long perfect neck. Her deeply bronzed skin refracted light. She smiled at me as we stepped toward the center of the room. About halfway across the space that divided me from sweet Cindi, the idea of touching her so scared me that I peed in my pants.

I tried to dance with her anyway.

I took her hand. She continued to smile, but then

squinched up her tiny nose and frowned. "What's that smell?" she said.

"I don't know," I said, and urine trickled down my legs and onto my shoes. I don't know if Cindi saw it. I turned and ran, shriveled and sloshing, from Miss Cederick's.

Every Wednesday afternoon for the rest of the year, as other kids refined their moves on the dance floor, I played alone under the railroad trestle across from the school, pretending that I was Muhammad Ali. I never told Daddy that I had quit going to Miss Cederick's.

Throughout my adolescence, my bedroom walls were covered with newspaper clippings of Ali's victories; yet when he lost to Joe Frazier in their first fight, I felt even closer to him. After all, hadn't life regularly kicked the shit out of me? And didn't that make me at least a little bit like Ali?

I especially liked an article that included a brief interview with Arthur Mercante, who had refereed the Frazier fight. Mercante said that Ali could've whupped Frazier if he hadn't elected to play around so much. Accompanying the article, there was a head-to-toe photograph of Ali spearing Frazier with a long, straight right, the oversized red and white tassels on Ali's shoes punctuating the beauty of his movement. I loved Ali for playing around. After all, I was the kind that seldom did what he was supposed to.

Years before, I had heard Ali tell the world, "No

Viet Cong ever called me niggah" and "I don't have to be who you want me to be." I read how he had thrown his 1960 Olympic gold medal into the Ohio River after not being allowed to eat in an all-white restaurant in Louisville.

I thought I knew something about what this must be like for Ali. Growing up in the South, in Winston-Salem, segregation had been an accepted way of life. "Colored folks" were required to sit in the back of buses, drink from "colored" water fountains, use "colored" restrooms; every fall, there was a county fair for the white citizenry and then the following week for "coloreds." Until my senior year in high school, I never went to school with anyone other than white kids.

I first came to care not only about compassion through Ali, but about the music of movement—and the music of language. Like my idol, I became clever with my tongue, learned to throw venom when I talked: "Gowna whup you so bad your own mama won't recognize you," I said, at first only to the mirror, but later half-jokingly to kids at school.

I'd get up in the middle of Spanish class, shop, or P.E. and demonstrate the way that Ali would destroy Frazier when they met again for the title. I'd be on my skates, prancing high and proud, in front of all the Mount Tabor crackers, circling to the left, then to the right; I'd stab the air with mercurial jabs and show how Ali would tie Frazier up in the clinches; "Shock 'em and lock 'em," I'd shout during my clinic. And not only did I not mind that the kids and the teachers were laughing at me; like Ali himself, I'd be fueled by their responses.

And I began to actually believe that I might just be able to kick ass, maybe.

Which makes me remember the first afternoon that I landed in the principal's office for fighting. A kid not too much bigger than me had walked up to my sister Carol and me in the lunch room and called Ali "a draft-dodgin' uppity nigger" right square to my face. He sneered and laughed, and I hit him, not only in defense of Ali and his beliefs, but in defense of my family pride.

"You boys get three licks for fighting," Mr. Marion, a square-bodied former Golden Gloves boxer, said as he pulled from a drawer of his desk a short flat wooden paddle with dime-sized holes all through it.

"Not me. You're not whippin' me," I told him. "Especially with that thing." I pointed at the paddle, wondering if the school system had issued it or if he'd made it himself, which seemed likely considering how ugly it looked.

Mr. Marion told my opponent to go out to the anteroom and, when the door to the office was closed, he asked for Daddy's work number and summoned his secretary on the intercom. Within fifteen minutes, there was a knock at the door. The secretary showed my father into the room.

Mr. Marion rose from behind his desk. The skin around Daddy's mouth was stretched tight, but always the optimist, he smiled when they shook hands. Daddy pulled a soft cotton handkerchief from his pants pocket and told me to wipe the dried blood from my mouth. "Did you start it?" he asked as he took a seat beside me on the small green sofa.

I told him truthfully that I hadn't.

I stared at my untried hands, palms soft and child-like, seldom-used fingers short and thin, nails perfect, then at my father's: his nails manicured like mine; his palms exactly the shape of my own but a little rough with old calluses; our fingers almost the same length and shape, but his thicker; the back of his right hand permanently ribboned with keloid scars from when it had been grabbed by one of the machines at the plant. And then I looked at his face. Saw his rule-straight, crow-black hair (not at all like the blondish brown curls that ride my head); smelled the Old Spice aftershave I had given him for Christmas; saw the deep furrows in the forehead above the cliff of bone that shadows his eyes and makes his brown irises look almost black; saw his high, dark cheeks, the flesh around them beginning to droop. With age? No, Daddy was still a young man; they drooped from work and worry. I had, in effect, not seen my father before that moment.

Daddy turned to Mr. Marion. "He didn't start it," my father said.

"Fighting's dangerous," the former Golden Glover replied. "The rules say he gets three licks."

"Nobody decides to whip my son but me," my father said. "And I don't whip him."

Daddy told Mr. Marion that he was taking me

home. As we left the office, the principal looked stymied.

At the house, Daddy sewed up holes in both my pants legs and gave me an ice pack so I could nurse my split lip and swollen jaw. He stayed home from work and fixed my favorite supper: pinto beans, stewed squash, fried okra, and cornbread. He stuffed his cornbread in a tall glass of sweet milk and spooned it into his mouth. I did too.

It wasn't long before I began trying to dress like Ali, often wearing all white or all black. I took two to three showers every day, washed my hair nightly, and each time I passed a sink I scrubbed my hands. I felt a need to remain spotless. Unsoiled. Clean, all the time.

I bought clothes with every penny that Daddy would give me. All my slacks had to be professionally dry-cleaned before I'd wear them. I refused to own jeans or T-shirts (even though they were the fashion at school), and I'd not allow a shirt on my back unless it had been heavily starched—the stiffer the shirt, the exoskeleton, the more substantial the man.

My senior year, black kids were bused in from the black high school on the east side of town. Many of the black guys dressed pretty much the way I did. Some of them called me "Little Big Man" and "Mr. Clean." I liked that. "Mr. Clean." And I liked the way they'd laugh, sometimes, when they called me that. "Mr. Clean," they'd say, and the laugh would just roll out, all by itself: slow and musky, full-throated and even kind of sympathetic. To a naive, desperate, and romantic kid, there was something warm and wise in the tone.

I began smoking cigars, fat ole stogies nearly twice as big around as my thumb. I sucked the smoke in and blew it out, the cigar hanging out of the corner of my mouth, my left arm hooked around a rolled-down car window, trying to look cool perched up high on the seat cushion that I needed to see over the steering wheel, even as the discharged smoke found its stinging way into my eyes. I bought cigars in big ten-cent packs that barely fit into the starched pockets of my size-fourteen boys' shirts. And I completed my look by wearing English-style Ben Hogan golf caps at the accepted cool Southern angle, brim high and slightly to the left of my nose, cap tilted fifteen degrees left of level.

From mid-1971 through 1972, as Ali whipped himself back into shape to reclaim his title from Frazier, he fought about once every six weeks. Most of his bouts were broadcast on ABC's *Wide World of Sports*. I built my whole week around the Saturdays when Ali fought. I read both the morning and afternoon newspapers every day. Information about Ali was the only interest I had in the papers. I even got Daddy to buy a subscription to *Sports Illustrated* just so I could study the Ali stories. I was surprised how little the newspaper and magazine writers seemed to understand about Ali. Although I couldn't manage to pass English, I figured I could write better stories about Ali than these guys.

I typically found the most substance not in the

texts of the articles, but in the accompanying photographs, in which Ali was invariably iridescent in action. I cut out the best Ali pictures and pasted them on a piece of black poster board, which I hung on the wall opposite my bed, where I'd see them each night before I went to bed and each morning when I woke.

Saturdays before an Ali fight, I'd be so nervous that I could hardly eat. I'd spend much of the afternoon pacing the rooms of the house, dancing in long elegant strides like Ali, up on the balls of my feet circling clockwise, stopping at every mirror to whirl into a flurry of pitty-pat punches, then dancing on to another room, maybe slowing every now and then to open the refrigerator and bubble a hit of Coke straight from the bottle. About an hour before fight time, I'd get so nervous that my formerly starch-stiff shirts would be limp and darkened with sweat. It wasn't uncommon to shower and change clothes a couple times on the afternoon of an Ali bout.

As *Wide World* came on at five, Ali was usually interviewed by Howard Cosell in the dressing room: "Just another day in the gym," Ali would say, taking remarkable pleasure simply in being Muhammad Ali, looking absolutely relaxed as he joked with Cosell and tugged at the front of the sportscaster's hairpiece: "Before I retire," he'd say, "I'm gowna own me that rug," and I wasn't relaxed at all: My stomach would be in a knot that felt exactly the size of what Daddy would've called a full-growed man's fist. But I loved it, every moment of it. Even the pain.

As soon as the opening bell rang and Ali danced toward the center of the ring and his opponent, my mind went clean. Watching Ali fight was about the only time that I felt I was living in the now, in the moment. For me, there was an immediacy unique to the Ali experience. I moved *inside* the elegance of his rhythm. A time distortion occurred—seconds felt like minutes, minutes became eternal.

And on Mondays at school, I'd hear the black students in the halls talking about how beautiful Ali had looked against Jimmy Ellis or George Chuvalo or Whomever. Listening to the blacks talk, I felt that I was part of some real (yet mysterious) community, that I was still inside the Ali rhythm.

"My man was a high steppin' razor," I remember one black Ali fan saying, his voice echoing from the walls as I passed him on the way to or from some long forgotten classroom. The reason I remember this fan in particular, and this moment, is because of the way he stood up for me in hygiene class.

I took hygiene because I could substitute it for a credit in P.E. (I wouldn't dress or undress in front of people, not even guys) and because the class was so easy. I think most other maladjusts took it for the second reason.

The hygiene teacher's name was Miss Crabb. I swear. Miss Crabb, trying to teach hygiene to an eighteen-year-old virgin who took three showers a day.

I had hygiene with Miss Crabb third period and, as was my ritual in all classes, I sat in the back of the room with the delinquents. King Mobely sat directly in front of me.

King's daddy was a Southern Baptist preacher, the Right Reverend Jimmie Lee Mobely, who'd been captain of the RJR football team sometime back in the forties. King carried on that tradition. He was one of the cocaptains for the 1971–72 school year. And King apparently picked up his daddy's style of speech, too. King didn't talk; he orated.

King was short, only a couple of inches taller than me, but he weighed about 185. He had a hard, square, flat face and wore his hair in the sort of fake-hip, plastered-down style you'd expect a TV weatherman to wear. And he always walked like he'd just stepped down from a horse. He shuffled along, stiff as pasteboard, shoulders hunched up high, arms stuck out from his sides a full ten degrees.

I admired and envied King's muscles and respected the work it took to pack all that apparent power into them. I wouldn't even have minded being friends with King. If only he hadn't tried so hard to be a mean ass. You could look at him and just tell he felt he *had* to live the role expected of a football captain and Southern Baptist. He had to hate little twerps like me and coons and Methodists and agnostics and anybody else who wasn't mostly like him, and his daddy.

Beside King, on my left, was Orpheus Jones, my number-one Ali fan. Or OJ, as his friends called him.

They could call him OJ all they wanted, but I thought Orpheus sounded better. I liked the name from the first time Miss Crabb had called roll.

King was yelling across the room, preaching for his buddy Skip Archley, who claimed to have downed thirty-six beers the night before and who was sitting slumped in the far corner, his head propped on his forearms, staring out the windows.

"Cain't be nobody needs to be on welfare," King declared. "Wallace'd put a stop to it for sure, if somebody'd only let him."

I tapped King on the shoulder. When he turned, I found myself distinctly mouthing the words, "George Wallace sucks."

King stuck out his chin and craned his head to the side. "Whaa?" he said.

"I said, 'Wallace sucks.'"

Everything stopped. Suddenly nobody was listening to Miss Crabb's lecture. King's jaw dropped, he stared, and I realized I had probably overcommitted myself. But I didn't know how to put on the brakes.

"You heard me," I heard myself say.

King slammed the back of his chair against the front of my desk and, remaining seated, grabbed for whatever sections of me he could separate from my body. Only I wasn't there. I had slid my chair away from him, against the wall, and I crossed my quaking legs, pulled my golf cap down over my eyes, and tried to put on a *So what?* Ali/world-slick kind of smile.

"And you know what, King?" I said, my voice shaking from under my cap. "You suck, too."

When I said that a bunch of stuff happened at once—King went flush and stood up, straddling his chair; the rest of the class turned around to laugh and gawk; Miss Crabb started out the door for the principal's office; King clenched his fists, began to shake; and Orpheus reached over, casually grabbed the back of King's lime-green Ban-Lon shirt, and sat him back in his seat.

King hoarsely screamed, "I'll kill you, you little sonofabitch."

And Orpheus wisely smiled and matter-of-factly said, "Don't be messin' with our little cuz, Chuck. He's a good man. Mr. Clean. You fuck with him, and we niggahs, we gonna dice and slice and Ronco Vegematize you."

"Wow," I said.

Not only was I thankful, I was impressed. There was a true rhythm to the way Orpheus had handled King. He'd made me feel like I might have some value to somebody after all. *We*, he had said, and *our* and *cuz* and *man* and *Mr. Clean*. Maybe I was right about there being some kind of community headed up by Ali. Maybe I stood half a chance of becoming more than a mere midget. It made me glad I did what I did. Even if I was still scared half to death of King.

The best thing that happened because of the incident in hygiene was that Orpheus and I became kind of tight. We began talking outside of class, about Ali and clothes and he of the ladies, and he invited me over to the "crib" he shared with his older brother. I could barely believe that someone my age already had his own apartment. And I'll never forget that the place smelled the way I believed bottom soil would smell if you could cook it. How rich and Dark and right that smell was to me. Yet, although I had a good time, I never went back. And though I remember the apartment well, and how special everything seemed there—the bright, ripe colors; the incensed air; the "sounds" on the stereo; the posters of Martin Luther King, the Kennedys, and Ali—I no longer remember what Orpheus looked like. But maybe that doesn't matter. Because I remember the song in his voice.

I bought an eight-track tape player for my car and, never having developed a taste for falsetto rock and roll, I drove down to Junior's Record Shop on North Trade Street—HOME OF THE *BLACKEST* VINYL, the sign read—and with money Daddy had been putting in my college savings account, I bought twenty soul and jazz tapes: Isaac Hayes and James Brown (which I'd heard at OJ's), the Four Tops and the Temptations, Aretha and Marvin Gaye, Stevie Wonder and the Isleys, Cannonball Adderley and Miles Davis, Curtis Mayfield and the Impressions, the Stylistics, the Delfonics, the Whispers.

Music at once raw and polished, rough and gentle, slick yet honest. Snakes on the riverbanks and sweet waters straight from the stream.

*   *   *

After flunking English a fourth time and making it up in summer school, I had the honor of graduating third from the bottom out of 1,473 students, the largest class in the history of the Winston-Salem/Forsyth County school system. In five years of high school, I had received only sixteen and one-half credits. It was supposed to take seventeen to graduate. The one-half I was missing was in physical education. Somebody in the office just didn't notice, or maybe they'd simply wanted to be done with me.

I told Daddy I didn't want to start college until second semester. I'd rather work for a few months and save some money, I lied. I didn't look for a job that fall because I didn't feel that I was good enough at anything that anybody would pay someone to do. I was more depressed than I had ever been. For months and months, I spent most of my time lying around the house moping and sleeping, wondering if there might be something I could do with my life.

All of that changed on Saturday, March 31, 1973. At four P.M., on a special live early edition of *Wide World of Sports*, Ali was to fight an ex-North Carolina-stationed Marine named Lenny somebody or other in Lenny's hometown. In a prerecorded interview, Ali promised Cosell (who, I'd learned in my reading, was born in Winston-Salem) that he was going to do some real pretty thumpin', even if he hadn't trained a single day, even if the right side of his jaw was still sore from having recently had two molars excised.

Ali entered the ring in a white, rhinestone-studded robe that had been given to him by Elvis Presley. The inscription PEOPLE'S CHAMPION had been embroidered across the shoulders. The stones on the robe flashed silver coins of light across the spectators in the ringside seats and into the lenses of the TV cameras. Yet Ali's body radiated no glow. His skin was splotched and had a greenish tint. At first I thought that the color needed adjusting on Daddy's new Japanese TV. Until I spun the channel selector and everybody looked fine everywhere else. I knew, then, that Ali would lose.

As he somnolently removed his robe, his weight was announced as 221, the second highest of his career; he looked bloated as a blowfish. The bell rang for Round One. The Man who had never missed a punch was suddenly missing them all. The Man who was always so full of himself was suddenly empty. After the second round, I couldn't watch any longer. I asked Daddy to tell me what happened and I left the room.

I ran to the basement and danced around the open cement floor, shouting "You gotta stick to win, Champ, gotta stick to win," my voice ricocheting hollowly off the concrete-block walls. I bruised the air with fast, slapping jabs, feeling a kinetic connection to Ali, as if some kind of long, nearly invisible tube existed between him and me. If I could get the juices flowing through my arms and legs, they'd have to be funneled, bubbling with power, through that tube and into him. The sleeves on my shirt made sharp, clean, good feeling, popping noises. I danced and popped and sweated real fine, then I couldn't not watch the fight and I ran up the stairs three at a time to find out how Ali was doing. It was Round Four. Daddy told me what I didn't want to hear. I plunged back down the stairs, sweated, snapped, and moved some more, then sprang up the steps again the fifth round, the eighth, the ninth, the eleventh, the twelfth, and, the last time, I stood in the den, skin cold with drying sweat, and saw Ali reel along all four sets of ropes, the whole right side of his face swollen and shining green under the television lights. I thought, or said, *No, this isn't happening; he's faking again,* but suddenly the round was over and so was the fight. Ken Norton had won by split decision. Or so the ring announcer said. I knew that Norton hadn't won; that, instead, Ali had lost: the distinction being that Ali had been defeated not so much by his opponent, but by what Ali himself hadn't done. Ali's longtime cornerman, moonfaced Drew "Bundini" Brown, cried as Ali left the ring. Ali didn't cry. He carried his head high and cocked to the left side. He didn't hide his pregnant dinner roll of a jaw. I stepped slowly and deliberately back to the basement, jaw set, head turned to the left.

For a straight half hour, I threw a punch every one-fourth second at the air in front of me, the hardest blows I had ever thrown, and forced my arms to keep pumping when they trembled and wanted to quit. For that half hour, I was a metronome on amphetamines. I wanted to become mechanical, soulless. I didn't want to think about Ali or myself or any fucking thing.

The next morning, I woke feeling settled, all cleaned out. Ali's mortality had been confirmed, and his jaw broken, by Ken Norton's fists. Maybe this wasn't so bad. Indeed, for me it was nothing less than a revelation. Muhammad Ali wasn't some kind of mutant, after all; he was a man. Just like me. Or the me I felt I was inside.

At thirty-one and on a slow slide down, if Ali were to retain the superiority he'd always had over his opponents, and a mastery of his body, he'd certainly have to change a few things. He said so himself, through clenched teeth and wired jaws, in an interview late the following week. It was the first time I'd heard effortless-looking Ali even talk about training.

"I want to thank Kenny Norton," he said. "Learned a very important lesson from him. From now on, I'll be a good old man. Like Archie Moore. I'll eat the right foods, run ten hard miles a day. Do thousands of sit-ups, hundreds of rounds of sparrin' and bag work. And you white folks'll find out what this old spade has left."

So. We would. Ali would not fold. He would not give in. And if he wouldn't, neither would I.

I asked Daddy if I could borrow the keys to the fishing trailer we kept at Emerald Isle. I drove to the coast by myself. I sat beside the water for two days and at night I walked on the pier. "Anything biting tonight?" I asked expressionless, stubble-faced fishermen. Sometimes there was, often there wasn't.

"These waters about fished out," one old fellow said. To his left stood a drunk kid about my age, who was tall and obese and held a big red fist tight around a nine-inch-long sand shark. "That'll teach you," he said to the shark, slapping its bloodied head against the top of the railing, then flipping it over the side of the pier.

By the time I drove home on the third day, I had decided to *do* something in this world, something important. If not important to anybody else, then at least important to me.

Two

Yᴏu want to do *what?*" Daddy said when I told him my plans.

"All I need is a year, Dad. To find out."

"Dad?" he repeated, incredulity rising in his voice. I always called my father "Daddy," but I'd been feeling real adult lately. And the situation merited the more mature phraseology.

"I feel a need to get clean, to find out where I fit. I'm almost twenty-one. I can't afford to waste any more time."

My father laughed softly. "I can't tell you what to do, son," he said. "You're a full-growed man."

"No, I'm not," I said. "But I want to be."

"And you can't grow up in college?"

"I don't think so. Maybe some people can. I guess some do. I don't know. But not me."

It was Sunday afternoon and Carol, Daddy, and I were sitting around the dinner table after having gorged ourselves on turkey, steamed carrots, and boiled potatoes. "Davis," my father said, and I quit talking. Daddy almost always called me "Dave," the last exception being when I'd told him I wasn't going to attend high-school graduation ceremonies.

Carol picked up dirty dishes, carried them to the sink. "Son," my dad said, "I promised your mother before she died that I'd see to it you got a college education. Now I don't know what I should say. I reckon I can tell you I adored your mother. More than loved, I worshiped. And before you say that don't have nothin' to do with what we're talkin' about, let me finish.

"I'd hate like hell to see you work some no-account second- or third-shift job most your life. I've had to, and it's all because I didn't get that piece of sheepskin that says I got the right to know somethin'. I just want to warn you, son—the business world is filled with people who act like machines. They spout The Company as gospel and they'll suck the blood out of you, if you let them, and leave you dry as kindlin'."

I remembered stories my grandfather had told me then: tales about eleven brothers and sisters, of orphanages, about brawling his way out of the "Children's Home" as a prizefighter and years spent as a merchant marine; tales of those times large as fables: stories of gold, of oranges and cinnamon, of storms, of shipwrecks, of ghosts; imagining high adventure in the stories when I'd heard them as a kid and not recognizing the bone-real work and pain. I remembered Granddaddy's other stories, too, ones about his son's baseball days and how Daddy'd been a talented enough player to have been offered full-ride college scholarships. And how Daddy chose to marry my mother instead.

Deeper than memory, I *knew* what it was like for Daddy after they'd married. I knew about four A.M.s and the three hundred newspapers Daddy delivered every day before he went to work for ten hours in a corrugated box plant. I remembered that when Daddy hugged me, he was almost always wearing sand-colored khaki uniforms with company patches on them. And I felt what it was like to be very young and to not understand the look on my father's boss's face when, after Daddy was promoted to foreman, he told that boss on a Saturday afternoon as he was showing me around the plant, giving me rides on the freight elevator and on forklifts, "I ain't gonna work 'em like the corrugators, Mr. Sloan." Meaning the men.

I knew about better jobs Daddy'd been offered in Texas and in other parts of North Carolina, positions he didn't take because, as Granddaddy explained, "You kids woulda had to moved."

And maybe this is one hokey thing to say, but on a Sunday afternoon in April 1973, for the first time in my life, I came to understand Daddy in some way other than as the four walls, the ceiling, and the floor around me, as my environment. I came to understand a little about who Daddy was and what he had done for me.

He didn't have to tell me that I had a home in his house as long as I wanted it; he'd already said so without saying it. He didn't have to say that he supported my decision; I understood that he did.

Daddy would never be Muhammad Ali or Johnny Unitas or Mickey Mantle, or any of the other folks people idolize and buy books about. He would not escort the sun across the sky, would not walk only where he wanted to go. But he would allow me the opportunity he'd not had—the chance to do something with life besides work some half-ass job.

"I'll make it, Dad," I said. And as I spoke, I felt memories loosen like silt in a spring rain, sliding off the banks and into the muddy waters of the creek behind my father's house.

Three

I had decided that I was going to become the greatest martial artist to walk the face of the earth.

I went into training in May 1973. Over the next months, I did tens of thousands of push-ups, sit-ups, leg raises, stomach crunches, stretching exercises, and the like. I jumped rope a minimum of a half hour and ran at least five miles a day, every day. By eating four full meals every sixteen hours and drinking a couple blenders of whole milk, ice cream, bananas, and Bob Hoffman's weight gain powder every afternoon, I pushed my weight all the way to 145.

I began to kickbox, combining the legwork of karate with the punches and movement of boxing. Patterning my martial arts style after Ali's boxing skills, I soon found a rhythm and a suppleness that I felt had been asleep inside me. I slid Stevie Wonder's

Innervisions and *Fullfillingness' First Finale* albums onto the turntable and as the music swirled through me, I practiced *Sansen-tsuki*, which translates as "fighting blow," the first punch kyokushinkai beginners are taught.

In traditional kyokushinkai, Sansen-tsuki is thrown from the full-frontal *hachiji-dachi* position, fists inverted and on the waist, legs spread so far apart it looks as if you're trying to straddle a set of railroad tracks. But I brought my hands up to shoulder height, and instead of keeping my fists closed tight like my karate *sensei* had taught me, I held my hands loose and open ever so slightly, like Ali's. I turned to the left to present a smaller target, tucked my chin in next to my shoulder, raised my right hand to ear level, dangled the left one at my side (jabs could be popped loose and snappy and much faster from waist height), stationed my legs a couple feet apart and bent them just a little at the knees.

Behind my Ali-like jab, I worked on slinging as many of the twisting Sansen-tsuki as I could in two seconds' time, concentrating on throwing the punches in unpredictable patterns. I bought a full-length mirror that I placed against a wall in the basement and spent more than an hour a day shadowboxing in front of it: dancing to the left, hands at my sides and palms open, stopping and sliding back to the right, whipping out a jab as I switched again to the left. Like Ali, with every punch I threw, I blew the air from my lungs with a short, hot *fuuh* sound.

Studying the way Ali punched, I developed a pre-

cise yet slippery kicking method, popping kicks in relaxed, syncopated rhythms. For hours a day, every day,
I'd dance and punch and kick and talk at the mirror,
attempting to emulate the noble melody that was
uniquely Ali's: "No contest, no contest," I'd shout, and
"Is that all you got?" I'd ask the mirror, thinking of
the reflected face and body not as my own, but as that
of Joe Frazier or the U.S. draft board that had caused
Ali to lose his title or the exotic, black-cloaked,
Japanese ninja assassins I had read about in the library. "All night long," I'd yell, and "Keep that poison
on him," I'd exclaim. "Put the key in the lock," I'd cry,
trying to make my voice sound as street-rich as Bundini's. With hands or feet or mouth, no matter how
difficult the skill or maneuver, I focused always on
making everything look effortless and beautiful.

As I continued to get big, Ali was losing weight.
When he outpointed Norton in a September re-
match, he weighed 212, the same weight at which he
had fought Sonny Liston in 1964. In January 1974,
Ali again weighed 212 when he fought Frazier for the
second time. It was a closed-circuit TV event and,
not being able to watch the fight live, I drove up and
down muddy, potholed roads and listened to a round-
by-round being broadcast by a New York radio station. I wept and cheered and beat the palms of my
hands against the steering wheel as the overwhelming
decision was announced. Some undefined yet real be-
lief, so deep that it felt innate, was confirmed for me
by Ali's triumph.

That October, as an eight-to-one underdog, Ali

dominated and knocked out the supposedly invincible George Foreman to recapture the world's heavyweight title; almost overnight, he became the most popular man on the planet. In December, inspired by Ali's success, I had my first professional fight. Hundreds of millions had cheered for Ali in his victory over age and Foreman; fifty folks watched me outpoint my opponent, a stiff, traditional *karateka* who seemed never to have seen a jab other than the ones that I bounced off his face. The guy was so easy to hit that I became bored in less than two rounds, and felt sorry for him by the middle of the third. Yet, I didn't have the meanness or the skill to put him away.

Over the next two years, I took six more bouts. I liked the daily rigorousness required of a professional athlete, loved the flow of combat (the rapture of the ring). The act of sparring was the very first thing I had found in my life that made me feel good. I never considered unarmed combat to be destructive or separative. For me, sparring was relating: It was marriage with another person, coming together and going away in the same moment; it was *of* the Tao. When I fought, the rest of existence seemed less real than that which was being experienced on the lighted canvas. Like my idol, I enjoyed the art of flamboyantly efficient movement and a sense of rapscallion play. I liked to outfinesse and outthink opponents and make them seem silly and clumsy (maybe as an attempt to make up for having felt so goofy and awkward as a child and adolescent), but I didn't like hurting anyone or getting hurt.

Unlike Ali, when an opponent put pressure on me, when it came time to dig deep, I didn't need the pain that badly. When it was imperative to keep going to the well, to believe, after bringing up an empty pail or two, that I had to keep going back until I reeled in a shining bucket of life-saving water, I just couldn't do it. In my entire time as a kickboxer, the only person or thing I ever really kicked shit out of was my own ego. But this was victory enough. Through the thousands of hours (millions of minutes, billions of seconds) I spent learning to box and to perform martial art, I began to wake, to feel for the first time that I was living in each moment. I became open to the possibilities and to the mysteries. Like Ali, I strove to become hard and soft, fast yet precise and careful, strong and graceful. Snow clouds, fog, wind, thunder, blue skies in February and in August, drizzle, hurricanes. For me, there was power and beauty in all weather.

By 1976, I realized that I didn't have all it takes to become a world champion, or even a particularly wonderful fighter. But my rather rarefied experiences in the martial arts had spoiled me—I felt that there was no way I could ever be content working a day-to-day, nine-to-five job. Or any kind of job. I wanted to be an artist, wanted to live the artist's life. I decided that I'd go back to school and that I'd study creative writing.

I'd first come to care about beauty and precision and dignity from watching Ali, and I hoped to manifest some of those ideals in literary prose. Ali taught a generation a new way to see not only boxing but the world. I wanted to tell that world about my experiences in the fighting disciplines.

On the first paper that I turned in for creative nonfiction class, the instructor commented, "You're a pretty good writer, but you'll be more readable if you come out of samurai training for a while."

These comments prompted me to drop his class, but I came back the following semester. In the interim, my ego had become a little less fragile to criticism: Whatever the cost, I wanted to do the best writing in me. Using the discipline, control, and puissance I had learned from the martial way and from Ali, I worked obsessively toward this goal. The voice of the street and of sky, of earth and of anima, would be in my work.

While in school, I sold a story to *Sports Illustrated* about my 1975 sparring experience with the Champ. I was so naive I thought this small success meant that I could quit college (for the betterment of my mind and spirit), spend six months writing a novel, go on the *Tonight Show*, and soon change the course of Western literature. Like my idol, I did not much value understatement. "I will become the greatest writer of all times," I said over and over in my very best Ali voice while standing in front of the bathroom mirror.

I worked part-time in music and book stores while I taught myself the craft of fiction writing. When everyone else forgot my one sell to the Mount Olympus of sports magazines, I reminded them. I submitted chapter after chapter of my novel to magazines, hoping and believing that some editor, somewhere, would publish them as excerpts; no one bought my stories. I eventually took a job managing a video store, which didn't mean that I had given up my dream; I had simply put it to sleep. "I'll get to it, I'll get to it," I told myself as I read other people's books while lying in bed each night.

I'm back at Reynolds High. In the hall outside the door marked PRINCIPAL. *Middle-aged now, but here I am, still a student. I've had to go back, to make up for all time uselessly spent.*

King Mobely is standing right in front of me, blowing Winston smoke in my face. And Mike Stone is slouching against a wall beside Lenny Lawsen, maybe the dumbest kid in school. Lenny Lawsen, the premier wrestler on the RJR squad, who spent every other weekend in jail as penalty for having been caught driving after his license had been revoked, who spelled Reynolds with an "i" instead of an "e," and who always called me stupid.

"Look at that stupid nigger-lookin' hair," he'd spit in spasms, or "that stupid Jewboy nose"; he'd laugh, sticking a couple of short, fat fingers onto my face and giving the cartilage a not-playful twist.

They're all here, and they're still seventeen. I'm in the middle of a circle they've formed around me. They move for me as one.

I slide toward Lawsen first, sidekick his thick, slow body into the wall about ten feet away. The kick flows out from the center of my abdomen, is explosive, and the moment of contact goes good and warm from foot up into hip. I step outside their circle, ready to whup 'em all. But from the principal's office steps—Ali! White on black pin-stripe suit, red silk tie. Captain Clean, as usual. His hand is as large as a paddle. He slaps all my enemies for me.

"Thanks, Champ," I say. He smiles his easy Ali smile and steps back through the office door. I know the perfect way to repay his kindness.

"I'll spank ole Smokin' Joe for you, Champ," I say, absolutely confident I can actualize my boast.

Every morning when I woke from my dreams, I went back to the store, to my role as video guru: I began to take pleasure in helping costumers find tapes that they wanted, even though the movies usually weren't ones that I liked. Charles Bronson and Burt Reynolds were big at my store, as were titles like *Women in Cell Block 9*, *I Dismember Mama*, and *Invasion of the Samurai Sluts from Hell*.

I enjoyed European films, particularly French romances and British comedies, and some American dramas. Several times a week, another person whose movie sensibilities were similar to my own came into the store. I liked to recommend tapes for these customers; folks often came again and again and asked me to choose movies for them. Although I knew damned well that my secret self, the one who mattered most to me, was detached, removed, and protected from all of this, customer relationships allowed me to tell myself that I was doing something that mattered, that I was making a contribution of some sort (no matter how small) to contemporary culture. I told myself that I enjoyed being in a business so young, vibrant, and alive that I could feel I was baking it fresh each day. I took pleasure in the small acts of creation that the job allowed.

It wasn't long before I came to like the store's clean, straight lines and angles—the simple sky-blue counters, the plastic mirrored slotwall, the thumping little CD player and huge TV monitors that kept the store humming. I thought our chain did the best-looking and -sounding and -feeling stores in the video business. I had a PA system installed in the store. On Friday and Saturday nights I told jokes and ran trivia contests. One of my favorite questions went something like "In February 1964, Cassius Marcellus Clay knocked out Sonny Liston to win the heavyweight championship of the world. The next day the new champion announced that he was Muslim and changed his name. The first person who steps up to the counter and tells me that name will win a certificate for five free rentals . . . courtesy of Video Village, the greatest movie store of all times."

People would scramble to the counter, believing that they knew the answer. Only once did someone guess that Clay changed his name first not to Muhammad Ali, but to Cassius X—and that person had heard me ask the question, and give the answer when no one could correctly guess it, a couple weeks before.

My in-store promotions were so successful that I was twice named store manager of the year; I came to see the store as my art, and my sport. I quit working out, started eating foods I never ate as an athlete, gained thirty pounds I didn't need. For the first time since my teen years, I didn't like the way my body looked. How awful it felt to be in the shower, to glance down and not receive immediate visual confirmation of my own maleness. I developed pains in my chest and lower abdomen and spent hundreds of dollars on diagnostic tests. When giving me results, doctors would chuckle and say things such as "Looks like you'll live a few years, son."

After a while, I almost managed to forget that I didn't really give a hoot about movies, about video, about television, about "new technologies"—and that I even considered them to be enemies of those things I most cherished: books, writing, the natural world, and unpressured time spent with the people closest to me.

In the fall of 1987, the company made me a regional manager and asked me to transfer to Louisville, Kentucky, where Ali had been born and grew up. I was thirty-five years old, married, and the father of two young children. I thought about Ali only occasionally; he had been a childhood obsession.

When I moved to Louisville, the owner gave me a tour of the stores that I would supervise. On the way to a location on the south side of town, he pointed across the street to a small red brick ranch and said, "Muhammad Ali's mom lives there." From then on, I radared in on the house whenever I passed by.

Shortly after leaving North Carolina, we scraped
up every nickel we could and put down payments on
a new Volvo station wagon and on a house in a
neighborhood on the banks of the Ohio River; it was
a place of great pastoral beauty near the edge of wild-
ness—we were enveloped by a parklike sense of shelter and innocence and play. In our neighborhood,
there were two hundred acres of common meadows,
woods, deer, bluebirds, boat docks, fishing lakes, a
swimming pool, tennis courts, horse stables. The
grass, even in winter, was a hue of green I'd not seen
anywhere else.

Our home was organic architecture in the truest
sense—a dwelling that felt of its surroundings, not
separate from them. Like the meadows around us,
rooms were spacious, empty, and alive with sunlight
at all times of day. The small stone fireplace in the
great room seemed a natural outcrop of the sun-
splashed, moss-bright, wet limestone cliffs to our
east. At night, Lyn and I watched the moon and stars
through the skylight in our bedroom. Every morning,
when we woke, we looked out the wall-sized window
beside the bed and peered through branches of river
birch at the deep, slow-moving, quarter-mile-wide
Ohio.

We were enraptured with the house, the chip-
munks in our downspouts, the rocks, the raccoons on
our deck, the meadows, the snow geese in the spring
and fall, even the flock of turkey buzzards that nested
in the towering sycamores down by the river—fright-
ful and hideous on the ground, shining and perfectly

majestic in flight. There was a sanctity to the very sound of our neighborhood. The silence around us seemed a miraculous insulation from what we regarded as the insanity of the late twentieth century, refuge from a culture that more and more regularly honored the crude, the obvious, the graceless—a society that was a Harley-Davidson crashed on its side with its throttle stuck open at full tilt.

On Sundays—the only day I usually didn't have to work more than a couple of hours—I'd walk down to the shore and stand and suck in the impossibly live smell of the river and imagine myself to be Mark Twain. The house and the whole area made me feel connected to the world in a way that seemed ancient, intrinsic, ancestral: It was the only place I had lived that I considered home.

The job itself was not such a source of pleasure. I managed nine stores, five in Lexington and four in Louisville. The Kentucky locations had been poorly supervised for years; they were the only nonprofitable stores in the chain. It was my mission to turn them around. The owner thought that I'd be able to accomplish this resurrection because I'd been so successful in my North Carolina store. My role as video messiah often required me to work more than eighty grinding hours a week. I was under constant pressure to bring the stores alive—I wore an electronic pager on my hip that seemed always to be beeping, no matter where I was or what I was doing. In these blue plastic stores, I couldn't have felt more artificialized; I felt as subjugated, as squashed, as a rodeo calf leapt upon by a hog-tying cowpoke.

The last week of March 1989, the owner asked me to drive up to the home office in Cincinnati, where I was told that over the next year the company would close all of its central Kentucky locations. "You had to know this was coming," he said, but I hadn't. I thought that the stores would be moved to better locations, not shut down. I was even counting on a raise that would make it easier to pay the bills, and was looking forward to the day that I could cut back to forty-hour weeks and get to see the ordinary miracles of my neighborhood in daylight hours.

Instead, I would soon be without a job. Lyn and I had a six-year-old daughter, a three-year-old son, monthly payments on the Volvo, a full-blown, full-time mortgage in paradise to support. With the money I made, it was a constant stretch to make ends meet. We had no one in Louisville we could call on for support; we were five hundred miles from our friends and family. I was scared, and when I told Lyn, she became frightened, too. Nearly every waking moment, I felt a flame of responsibility and an icicle of fear in the pit of my stomach.

On Good Friday, April 1, 1989, two days before Resurrection Day, I was on the way to my southside Louisville store. As always, I looked to the right as I passed Ali's mother's place. A block-long white Winnebago with Virginia plates was parked on the grass. I knew it was his vehicle.

Since 1962, when he has traveled unhurried, he has

driven buses or RVs. And he owned farmland in Virginia. The connections were obvious. I drove past the house, worked up courage, turned around, came back. I parked the Volvo behind the Winnebago and grabbed a few old magazines I'd been storing under the front seat ever since moving to Louisville, waiting for the meeting with Ali I'd been sure would come.

When I thought of Ali, I remembered him as I'd seen him at his training camp all those years before. Yes, in those days he had been luminous with sweat and hubris. His hands and feet seemed to be constantly moving in almost impossibly wondrous patterns and his eyes shone like electric blackberries. But every recent report had Ali sounding like a turtle spilled onto his back, limbs thrashing air.

I was sure he wouldn't remember me; he had met, and sparred with, nearly half the population of the planet. But I'd always believed that, given the chance to sit and talk with him for a long time, he and I would become friends.

When I rang the bell, his younger brother Rahaman opened the door. He saw the stack of magazines under my arm, smiled an experienced smile, and said, "He's out in the Winnebago. Just knock on the door. He'll be happy to sign those for you."

Rahaman was much as I remembered him from seventies' TV screens: tall as his brother, mahogany skin, and a mustache that helped him look like a cross between footballer Jim Brown and a black, aging Errol Flynn. There was no indication in his voice or on his face that I would find his brother less than healthy.

I recrossed the yard, climbed the couple of steps on the side of the Winnebago, and prepared to knock. Ali opened the door before I got the chance. I'd forgotten how damned big he is. His presence filled the doorway. He leaned under the frame to see me.

I felt no nervousness. Ali's face, in many ways, is as familiar to me as my father's. His skin remains unmarked, his countenance has a near-perfect symmetry. Yet something is different: He's no longer the world's prettiest man. He remains handsome, but in the way of a youngish granddad who likes to tell stories about how he could have been a movie star, if he'd wanted. And he carries himself with the wisdom that granddads have in the movies. His pulchritude used to challenge us; now he looks a bit more like us, and less like an avatar sent by Allah.

"Come on in," he says, and waves me past. His voice has a gurgle to it, as though he needs to clear his throat. He offers a massive hand. He does not so much shake hands as he places his hand in mine. His grip is hardly a grip at all—his touch is gentle as a girl's. His palm is cool and uncallused; his fingers are the long, tapered digits of a hypnotist; his fingernails look professionally manicured. His knuckles are large and slightly swollen, as if he recently has been punching the heavy bag.

He is dressed in white, all white. New leather tennis shoes, thin over-the-calf cotton socks, custom-tailored linen slacks, and thick short-sleeve safari shirt crisp with starch. I tell him white is a better color for him than the black he usually wears these days.

He motions for me to sit, but doesn't speak. His mouth is a little tense at the corners; it looks like a kid's who has been forced by a parent or teacher to keep it closed. He slowly lowers himself into a chair by the window. I take a seat across from him and lay my magazines on a table between us. He picks them up, produces a ballpoint pen, and begins signing. He asks, "What's your name?" and I tell him. Without looking up, he continues to write. His eyes are not glazed, as I've read, but they look tired. A wet cough rattles in his throat. His left hand trembles almost constantly. Amid the silence in which we sit, I feel a need to tell him some of the things I've wanted to say for years.

"Champ, you changed my life," I say. "When I was a kid, I was messed up, couldn't even talk to people. No kind of life at all."

He raises his eyes from an old healthy image of himself on a magazine cover.

"You made me believe I could do anything," I say.

He's watching me while I talk, not judging, just watching. I pick up a magazine from the stack in front of him. "This is a story I wrote for *Sports Illustrated* while I was in college," I say. "It's about the ways you've influenced my life."

"What's your name?" he asks again, this time looking right at me. I tell him. He nods. "I'll finish signing these in a while," he says, putting his pen on the table. "Read me your story."

"You have a good face," he says when I'm through. "I like your face."

He'd listened seriously as I'd read, laughing at the funny lines and when I'd tried to imitate his voice. He had not looked bored. It's a lot more than I could have expected—Muhammad Ali often has a short attention span, but he had listened to, and seemed to enjoy, my story about him.

"You ever seen any magic? You like magic?" he asks.

"Not in years," I say.

He stands and walks to the back of the Winnebago, moving mechanically. It's my great-grand-father's walk. He motions for me to follow. There's a sad yet lovely, noble, and intimate quality to his movements.

He does about ten tricks. The one that interests me the most requires no props. It's a simple deception. "Watch my feet," he says, standing about eight feet away, with his back to me and his arms perpendicular to his sides. Then, although he's just had real trouble walking, he seems to levitate about three inches off of the floor. He turns to me and in his thick, slow voice says, "I'm a *baaadd* niggah."

I laugh and ask him to do it again; it's a good one. I think I might like to try it myself, just as fifteen years earlier I had taken a big cotton laundry bag, filled it with rags, and hung it from a ceiling beam in the basement. I pulled on a pair of Daddy's old brown work gloves and pushed my fists into that twenty-pound marshmallow two hundred, five hundred, a thousand times a day, concentrating on speed: dazzling, crackling speed, in pursuit of godly speed, trying to whip out punches so fast they'd be invisible to opponents. I got to where I could shoot six to eight crisp shots a second—"Shoe shinin'," Ali called it—and I strove to make my fists move quicker than thought, like Ali's; I sprang up on my toes, as I had watched Ali do; I tried to fly like Ali, bounding around the bag and to my left.

After the levitation trick, Ali grabs an empty plastic milk jug from a counter beside the sink. He asks me to examine it. "What if I make this rise up from the sink this high and sit there? Will you believe?"

"I'm not much of a believer these days, Champ," I say, thinking not only about the way my life is going, but also that part of what Muhammad Ali's malady teaches is that no one can defy gravity.

"Well, what if I make it rise, sit this high off the ground, then turn in a circle?"

"I'm a hard man to convince," I say.

"Well, what if I make it rise, float over here to the other side of the room, then go back to the sink and sit itself back down? Then will you become one of my believers?"

I laugh and say, "Then I'll believe."

"Watch," he says, then points at the plastic container and takes four steps back. I try to see both the milk jug and Ali. He waves his hands a couple times in front of his body. The container does not move from the counter.

"April Fools'," Ali says. We both chuckle and he walks over and slips his arm about my shoulders.

He autographs the magazines and writes a note on a page of my *SI* piece. "To Davis, The Greatest Fan of All Times," he writes, "From Muhammad Ali, 4-01-89." I feel that my story is finally complete, now that he has confirmed its existence. He hands me the magazines and asks me into his mother's house. We leave the Winnebago.

I unlock the Volvo and lean across the front seat, carefully placing the magazines on the passenger's side, not wanting to take a chance of damaging them or leaving them behind. Suddenly there's a cricket-like chirping noise in my ear. I jump back, swat the air, turn around. It was Ali's hand. He's standing right behind me. He has always been a big practical joker.

"How'd you do that?" I say. It's a question I've found myself regularly wanting to ask Ali.

He doesn't answer. Instead, he raises his fists to shoulder height and motions me out into the yard. We walk about five paces, I put up my hands, and he tosses a slow jab at me. I block and counter with my own. Fighters and ex-fighters always throw punches at each other or at the air or at trees or at whatever happens to be around. It's the way we play. Even now, working almost all the time and being absolutely out of shape, I still throw over a hundred jabs a day.

Surely Ali does, too. He and I had both stopped our punches a full foot from the other, but my adrenal gland is pumping at high gear from being around Ali and my jab had come out fast—it had made the air sing. He slides back a half step and takes a serious look at me. I can't help but flash back on our meeting from so many years before; I figure I'm going to get it now. A couple kids ride past on bikes. They recognize Ali and stop.

"He doesn't understand I'm the Greatest of All Times," he yells to the kids. He pulls his watch from his arm, sticks it in his pants pocket. I slip mine off, too. He'll get down to business now. He gets up on his skates and dances to his left a little, loosening his legs. Just a couple minutes before, climbing down the steps of his Winnebago, he'd moved so awkwardly he'd almost lost his balance. I'd wanted to give him a hand, but knew not to, having seen old Joe Louis "escorted" in that fashion; I couldn't do that to Muhammad Ali. But now that Ali is on his toes and boxing, he's moving pretty fluidly.

He flings another jab in my direction, a second, a third. He isn't even a quarter as fast as he had been in 1975, but his eyes are alert, shining like black marbles, and he's real relaxed and sees everything. That's one of the major reasons old fighters make comebacks: We are more alive when boxing than at most any other time. The grass around us is green and is getting high; it will soon need its first trim. New leaves look wet with the sun. A bluejay squawks from an oak to the left; six robins roam the yard. I instinctively block and/or slide to the side of all three of Ali's punches and immediately feel guilty about it, like being fourteen years old and knowing for the first time that you can beat your dad at Ping-Pong. I wish I could've stopped myself from slipping Ali's jabs, but reflexive training runs faster and deeper than thought. I zip a jab to his body, one to his nose, drop a straight right to his chin, and am dead certain all three would have scored. A couple cars stop in front of the house. His mom's is on a corner lot. Three more are parked on the side.

"Check out the left," I hear a young-sounding voice say from somewhere. I know the owner of the voice is talking about my punch, not Ali's.

"He's in with the Triple Greatest of All Times," Ali shouts. "Gowna let him tire himself out. He'll get tired soon."

I don't, but pretend to anyway. "You're right, Champ," I tell him, and drop my hands. "I'm thirty-seven. Can't go like I used to." The truth is, I probably could do three to four fairly hard rounds. I know how to pace myself pretty well.

I hold my right hand to my chest, acting out of breath. I look at Ali; his hand is in exactly the same position. We're both smiling, but he's sizing me up a little.

"He got scared," Ali yells.

Onlookers laugh from their bicycles and through car windows. Someone blows his horn and shouts, "Hey, Champ!"

"Come on in the house," Ali says softly in my ear.

We walk toward the door, Ali in the lead, moving woodenly through the new grass, while behind and around us people roll up their windows and start their engines.

Four

———————

"Gowna move back to Loovul, just part-time."

The deep Southern melody rolls sleepily in Ali's voice. His words come scarcely louder than a whisper and are followed almost immediately by a short fit of coughing.

Back to Loovul. Back to hazy orange sunsets and ancestors' unmarked graves; back to old slow-walking family (real and acquired), empty sidewalks, nearly equatorial humidity, and peach cobblers made by heavy, round-breasted aunts wearing flowered dresses; back to short, thin uncles and their straw hats, white open-collared shirts, black shiny pants, and spit-shined black Florsheims; back to a life that hasn't been Ali's since he was eighteen years old.

We're standing in the "family room," a space so dark I cannot imagine the drapes ever having been drawn, a room furnished with dented gold-painted furniture, filled with smells of cooking meat, and infused with a light like that of a fireplace fire.

Ali has just introduced me to his mother, Mrs. Odessa Clay, and to Rahaman, then suddenly he's gone.

Ali's family easily accepts me. They're not surprised to have a visitor and handle me with ritualistic grace and charm. Rahaman tells me to make myself at home, offers a root beer, and goes to get it. I take a seat on the sofa beside Ali's mother.

Odessa Clay is in her seventies, yet her face has few wrinkles. She is short, her hair is nearly as orange as those Louisville sunsets; she is freckled, pretty, and as fragile as my mother in her homecoming picture. Ali's face is shaped much like his mom's. While he was fighting, she was quite heavy, but over the past ten years she has lost what looks to be about seventy-five pounds.

She's watching *Oprah* on an old floor-model TV. I wonder where Ali has gone. Rahaman brings the drink and a paper napkin and a coaster. Mrs. Clay pats me on the hand. "Don't worry," she says. "Ali hasn't left you. I'm sure he's just gone upstairs to say his prayers."

I hadn't realized my anxiousness is showing. But Ali's mother has watched him bring home puppies hundreds of times during his forty-seven years. "He's always been a restless man, like his daddy," she says. "Can't ever sit still."

She speaks carefully, with a mother's sweet sadness

about her. The clip to her voice must once have been affected, but after cometing all over the globe with Ali, its inflections sound authentically British and Virginian.

"Have you met Lonnie, his new wife?" she asks. "Ali's known her since she was a baby. I'm so happy for him. She's my best friend's daughter, we used to all travel to his fights together. Since she was six years old, she always said she was going to marry him. She's a smart girl, has a master's degree in business. She's so good to him, doesn't use him. He told me, 'Mom, Lonnie's better to me than all the other three put together.' She treats him so good. He needs somebody to take care of him."

Just then, Ali comes back to the room, carrying himself high and with stately dignity, though his footing is ever so slightly unsteady. He falls deep into a chair on the other side of the room.

"You tired, baby?" Mrs. Clay asks.

"Tired, I'm always tired," he says, then rubs his face a couple times and closes his eyes.

He must feel me watching or is simply conscious of someone other than family being in the room. His eyes aren't closed ten seconds before he shakes himself awake, balls his hands into fists again, and starts making typical Ali faces and noises at me—sticking his teeth out over his lower lip, looking fake-mean, growling, other playful cartoon kid stuff. After a few seconds he asks, "Y-y-you okay?" He's so difficult to understand from across the room that I don't so much hear him as I conjecture what he must be saying. "Y-y-you need anything? They takin' care of you?" I assure him that I'm fine.

He makes a loud clucking noise by snapping his tongue across the roof of his mouth. Rahaman comes quickly from the kitchen. Ali motions him close and whispers briefly in his ear. Rahaman goes back in the kitchen. Ali turns to me. "Come sit beside me," he says, patting a bar stool to his right. He waits for me to take my place, then says, "You had any dinner? Sit and eat with me."

"Can I use the phone? I need to call home and let my wife know."

"You got kids?" he asks. I tell him I have two. He asks how old. I tell him the ages.

"They know me?" he asks.

"Even the three-year-old. He throws punches at the TV whenever I play your fights."

He nods, gratified. "Bring 'em over Sunday," he says. "I'll do my magic for 'em. Here's my mother's number. Be sure to call first."

I phone Lyn and tell her where I am and what I'm doing. She doesn't seem surprised. She asks me to pick up a gallon of milk on the way home. I know she's excited for me but we've got a lot of history together, some of it rough. In 1981, six weeks after our daughter was born, Lyn moved back in with her parents and divorced me because I wouldn't find a full-time job; that's when I was first learning how to write, thought success was imminent, and felt protected, even holy. Much of the time, I was walking about a yard above the ground—I believed nothing could possibly go wrong for Lyn and me; what *We* had was so rare that the universe would surely take care of us.

She'd been telling me for months that I needed a real job, something that would give us more money than the sixty dollars a week I brought home clerking a few hours in a bookstore. But I was driven with teaching myself to write, and I worked night and day, snatching every moment I could to dance the two-finger strut on the ancient typewriter my mother had used in secretarial school. And I denied myself, denied Lyn, denied our baby. (We lived in an apartment where nothing we did, including placing saucers of water under all four legs of the hand-me-down crib, prevented cockroaches from crawling into bed with our daughter.) I couldn't hear Lyn until it was too late and she was gone.

Her leaving was the reason I took a job in video; I still believed I'd make it as a writer, but desperately wanted her back and needed to show her that I was responsible. Lyn and I married for the second time just before we moved to Louisville. Although our getting back together seems like some sort of affirmation, with my current job situation she's not about to allow herself to gush like a schoolgirl over my spending time with Muhammad Ali.

When I hang up the phone, Ali asks about my wife. I tell him about our obsessive romance and that in 1977 we tried to get married at his fight with Earnie Shavers. I tell him that I met Lyn at a party after one of my bouts. What I can't tell him (but

what's with me as I speak) is that Lyn was seventeen
and I was a young twenty-four; she would become
my first girlfriend.

It was during the Christmas holiday of 1976 and it
was snowing, coming down in gobs the size of silver
dollars. As I stepped in from the snow, hands came
over to me, and faces, smiling, beaming faces, offering
congratulations. I took a seat on a sofa, one of those
overstuffed monsters that feel like they're going to
swallow you whole. And hands were on me, and faces
were full and wide with vicarious pride. The noises
that came from the faces were as indecipherable as a
session at the United Nations during an interpreters'
strike. Then Music sat beside me and I sank even
deeper into my seat.

"My name is Lyn," she said, and she brushed
melting snow from my hair. I stared at her, and
found it difficult to think. She had big brown animal eyes, high cheekbones, mane-thick, curly
auburn hair that tumbled more than halfway down
her back, and a dancer's long-waisted musculature.
She wasn't wearing makeup, and she didn't need
any. She was dressed in jeans that had holes in the
knees, a men's red flannel shirt, the top three buttons of which were undone. I can still see that shirt
as clearly as my own hands. She was wearing a
thermal long john T-shirt underneath. She looked
very physical, as if she had just come from climbing
trees, chopping wood, running naked through a
creek. The other girls in the room seemed silly next

to Lyn: They were too decked out in uptown
dresses or slacks and heavy, tacky jewelry; their
faces looked like they'd gotten made up at the corner bakery, like apple pies with too much flour on
their crusts.

"Will you teach me?" she said. Her eyes were huge
and molten and I understood she meant that she
wanted to learn the martial arts, but I heard other
connotations. It was exactly the time in my life when
I first knew that I was ready to be in love. This was
the girl I'd always believed I'd meet, the one who
would know what I knew, would be able to love in
the ways that I could, would understand all the things
I knew other men did not understand, but which
women did. The only one who could speak the language I did, the one who would make everything
come together, the one who'd make my life make
sense, because I was with her.

Before I'd met Lyn, what I'd thought I wanted was
to glow, alone, finished, under the light. Now I
wanted to throw myself completely away. I wanted to
crawl up inside her, wanted to breathe the air she
breathed, wanted to see the world she saw.

When Lyn and I started dating, I almost immediately quit doing martial art; ambitions that had
seemed so substantial faded into shadow (though I
would sometimes be haunted by them in dreams). I
just about stopped eating, I longed so to be with her.
More than longed, I felt I *had* to spend each waking
and sleeping moment with Lyn. Time with her was
so hearts-and-bones real that fantasies became in-

creasingly colorless and almost ceased to exist. We lived at such a high burn that both of us lost weight; she dropped from 105 pounds to 93, I fell to 118, though I hadn't ever been hungrier or healthier or happier than I was then. I wrote long letters to her every day. "When I'm not with you," I wrote, "it hurts to breathe." Lyn planned to go to college as an art major and to be a painter; I decided to enter school with her and to study creative writing.

In September 1977, near the beginning of our first semester at East Carolina University, I packed the car with clothes for Lyn and me, picked her up from her noon class, and drove straight to the bank, where we withdrew all of the money our parents had given us for the semester. "Terry, sorry I'm not in class today," began the note I left on my writing instructor's office door. "I've taken my girlfriend to New York to see the Muhammad Ali–Earnie Shavers fight. Oh, we're also going to get married while we're there. See you next week. Davis."

I'd always wanted to watch an Ali fight in person. And there wasn't much time left to do so. By the late seventies, Ali was barely able to shake beauty from his marrow and into his limbs. He often laid against the ropes and let fighters of lesser talent pound away at the Great Shrine, showing all of us that he was the Greatest Punching Bag of All Times, that we mortals couldn't possibly hurt the child of Allah.

"From now on," he said time and again in the final ring years, "I'm just gonna do what I gotta do to get by. Don't have to train to fight a few seconds in each round. And that's all it takes for me to whup most men."

To me, this seemed an almost conscious death wish. The last time we'd heard such talk from a public figure was at Gethsemane: "The cup that my Father hath given me, shall I not drink it?"

Lyn and I drove straight through the night, arriving in Manhattan the morning of the bout. As we checked into our motel, Lyn put on the wedding band that I had purchased months before. At a shop in the Waldorf-Astoria, she bought a simple jade ring for me. As we were leaving the hotel, we saw Ali on the street. More than ten thousand of us followed him as he walked to Madison Square Garden for the weigh-in. Traffic stopped in all directions. Although several people near Ali were taller and weighed more than he, he looked bigger than anyone I had seen in my life. There was a silence around him. As if his very skin were listening. There was pushing and shoving near the outside of the circle of people around Ali. Lyn and I stood on a concrete wall above and away from the clamor and looked down on him. There was a softness, a quietude, near the center of the circle; those closest to Ali were gentle and respectful.

That night in the Garden was the first time I had seen twenty thousand people move as one organism. The air was alive with the smells of pretzels and hot dogs, beer and marijuana. It was Ali's last good fight. He was regularly hurt by Shavers and would later say that Shavers had hit him harder than anyone ever. So resounding were the blows with which Shavers tagged Ali that Lyn and I heard them, the sound arriving what seemed a full second after we saw the punches connect, as we sat a quarter of a mile from the ring up in the cheap-seats stratosphere. In Round Fifteen, we were all standing and not realizing we had stood. I was trembling and Lyn was holding my hand and thousands of us were chanting "*Ahh-lee, Ahh-lee,*" his name our mantra, as his gloves melded into vermilion lines of tracers and the leering jack-o'-lantern opponent finally bowed before him.

The next morning, after watching Ali hold forth on the *Today Show* and checking out of our motel, Lyn and I went to get a marriage license. That's when we discovered that there was a three-day waiting period. We had spent all but forty dollars of our money at the fight, on the motel, and on my wedding band. We couldn't afford to stay; she was very disappointed. All during our long drive back to North Carolina, she was silent and hung her head. When she'd started college, I'd known that it was the first time she'd been away from her parents' house for longer than a weekend. What I hadn't recognized was how unformed she was, how young emotionally. She'd seemed so tough—it surprised me that she depended on me even more than I did on her. This was the first time she had seen me fail; I'm sure she's never gotten over it, even now. I was disappointed, too, but remained certain that she would soon cut loose, beyond the pull of gravity; she would become the ballsy, happier, primal-woods creature she really was inside.

She moved into my off-campus apartment and for the rest of the year neither of us was able to find a job; we had to live off of what little money I was able to make modeling for art classes at the university. Even though I was certain that everything would work out fine, for Lyn it was a horrible time. I'd come in from classes and find her in tears, worrying about what her parents would do when they found out she'd blown their money and was living with me. She eventually quit school because she couldn't buy materials for her art classes. It would be nearly a year before we felt we could afford to get married. Every weekend, to pay our electric bills, we filled cotton laundry bags with soft drink bottles we picked up beside highways. But, all these years later, I think we'd both do it the same way to see Ali in one of his last fights.

Now Rahaman brings two large bowls of chili and two enormous slices of bread from Mrs. Clay's kitchen. Ali and I sit at our chairs, take spoons in our hands. He puts his face down close to the bowl and the food is gone. Three minutes tops.

I continue to eat, and he speaks easily to me. "I remember what it was like to meet Joe Louis and Rocky Marciano for the first time," he says. "They were my idols. I'd seen their fights and faces so many times I felt I knew them. Want to treat you right, don't want to disappoint you.

"Do you know how many millions of people in the world would like to have the opportunity you're getting, how many people would like to come into my house and spend the day with me? Haven't fought in seven years and still get over four hundred letters a week."

I ask how people get his address.

"I don't know," he answers, looking puzzled and shaking his head. "Sometimes they come addressed 'Muhammad Ali, Los Angeles, California, USA.' Don't have a house in L.A. no more. Letters still get to me.

"When I move back to Loovul, gowna get me a place, a coffee shop, where I can give away free coffee and doughnuts and people can just sit and talk, people of all races, and I can go and talk to people. Have some of my old robes and trunks and gloves around, show old fight films, call it Ali's Place."

"I'd call it Ali's," I say, not believing there would or even could be such a place, but enjoying sharing his dream. "Just Ali's, that's enough."

"Ali's?" he repeats, and his eyes focus inward.

"People would know what it was," I say.

After a few seconds, I ask if he has videotapes of his fights. He shakes his head no. "Well, look," I say, "I manage a bunch of video stores."

"You're rich," he says, pointing and chuckling, but also being serious.

"No, no, I'm not. I just make a living. Look . . . why don't we go to one of my stores and get a tape of your fights, and we can watch it tonight. Would you like that? You want to ride with me?"

"I'll drive," Ali says.

There's a rubber monster mask in the Winnebago and I wear it on my hand on the way to the store, pressing it against the window at stoplights. A couple times people see the mask, then recognize Ali, who's wearing glasses as he drives. When he sees someone look at him, he carefully removes his glasses, places them in his lap, makes his hands into fists, and puts them beside his head. People point and lay on their horns and wave and cheer and shriek and lean out of their windows.

The store employees act as if they've been stricken dumb. When I visit a store, they typically ask for advice or tell me about problems they're having. This time, they stay away and simply stare at Ali. We borrow a Godzilla movie Ali wants to see and a tape of fight highlights and interviews called *Ali: Skills, Brains and Guts* that was written and directed by Jim Jacobs, the international handball champion and fight historian. Jacobs recently died of a degenerative illness. Ali doesn't know of Jacobs's death until I tell him.

"He was a good man," Ali says. "Did you know Bundini died?" he asks, speaking in the same tone he would use with a friend of many years. I feel very honored by his intimacy and tell him that I've heard.

In the Winnebago on the way back to his mom's,

he says, "You're sincere. After thirty years, I can tell. I feel it rumblin' up from inside people."

"I've learned a lot about kindness from you," I say. And: "I know a lot of people have tried to use you."

"They *have* used me. But it don't matter. I don't let it change me."

I stop by the Volvo again on the way into Mrs. Clay's house. There's one more picture I hope Ali will sign, but earlier I had felt I might be imposing on him. It's a head shot in a long-out-of-print biography by Wilfrid Sheed, a beautiful book that features hundreds of color plates. I grab the bio from the car and follow Ali into the house.

When we're seated, I hand it to him, and he signs the picture on the title page. "To Davis Miller, From Muhammad Ali, King of Boxing," he writes, "4-01-89."

I'm about to ask if he'd mind autographing the photo I especially want, but he turns to Page Two, signs that picture, then the next page and the next. He continues to sign for probably forty-five minutes, writing comments about opponents ("Get up Chump," he writes beside a classic photo of the fallen Sonny Liston), parents, Elijah Muhammad ("The man who named me"), Howard Cosell, spouses ("She gave me Hell," he scrawls across his first wife's picture), then passes the book to his mother and brother to autograph a family portrait. He even signs "Cassius Clay" on several photos from the early sixties. He flips twice through the book, autographing nearly every photo, pointing out annotations as he writes.

"Never done this before," he says. "Usually sign one or two pictures."

As he turns from page to page, he studies, then chooses not to autograph, a youthful picture of himself with the Louisville Sponsoring Group, the collective of rich white businessmen who owned his contract (and reportedly those of several thoroughbred racehorses) until he became Muslim. He also hesitates over a famous posed shot that was taken for *Life* magazine in 1963, in a bank vault. In this photo a wide-eyed and beaming Cassius Clay sits atop a million one-dollar bills. Ali turns to me and says "Money don't mean nothin'," and leafs to a picture with Malcolm X, which he signs, then poses his pen above the signature, as if prepared to make another annotation. Suddenly, though, he closes the book, looks at me dead level, and holds it out at arm's length with both hands. "I'm giving you somethin' very valuable," he says, handing me the biography as if deeding me the book of life.

I stare at the book in my open palms and feel that I should say something, that I should thank him in some way. I carefully place it on a table, shake my head slightly, and clear my throat, but find no words.

Five

I excuse myself to the bathroom, locking the door behind me. A pair of Ali's huge black shoes is beside the toilet. The toe of one has been crushed, the other is lying on its side. When I unlock the door to leave, it won't budge. I can't even turn the handle. After trying several times, I tentatively knock. There's laughter from the other room. I distinctly hear Mrs. Clay's and Rahaman's voices. I yank fairly hard on the door a few times. Nothing. Just when I begin to think I'm stuck in Odessa Clay's bathroom for the duration, the door easily opens. I catch a glimpse of Ali bounding into a side room to the right, laughing and high-stepping like some oversized, out-of-shape Nubian leprechaun.

I peek around the corner. He's standing with his back flat against the wall. He sees me, jumps from the room, and tickles me, a guilty-little-kid smile splashed across his features. Next thing I know, he has me on the floor, balled up in a fetal position, tears flowing down both sides of my face, laughing. Then he stops tickling me and helps me to my feet. Everybody keeps laughing. Mrs. Clay's face is round and wide with laughter. She looks like the mom of a Celtic imp.

"What'd you think happened to the door?" Rahaman asks. I tell him I'd figured it was Ali. "Then why you turnin' red?" he wants to know.

"It's not every day," I say, "that I go to Muhammad Ali's, he locks me in the bathroom, then tickles me into submission."

Everyone laughs again. "Ali, you crazy," Rahaman says.

Suddenly I realize the obvious, that I've been acting like a teenage admirer again. And that Muhammad Ali has not lost perhaps his highest talent—the ability to transport people past thoughts and words to a world of play. Being around Ali, or watching him perform on TV, has always made me feel genuinely childlike. Today, I'm not troubled at all by my own problems. I look at his family: They're beaming. Ali still flips their switches, too.

He trudges off to the bathroom right after helping me up. Rahaman creeps over from his seat on the sofa and holds the door, trying to keep Ali in. The brothers push and tug on the door and, when Ali gets out, laugh and wrestle around the room. Then Ali throws several feathery punches at Rahaman and a few at me.

We finally slip the Ali tape into the VCR. Rahaman brings everyone another root beer and we settle back to watch, he to my left, Ali beside me on the right, and Mrs. Clay beside Ali. The family's reactions to the tape are not unlike those you or I would have looking at old home movies or high-school yearbooks. Everyone sighs and their mouths arc at tender angles. "Oh, look at Bundini," Mrs. Clay says, and "Hey, there's Otis," Rahaman offers.

When there's film of Ali reciting verse, everyone recites with him. "Those were the days," Rahaman says several times, to which Mrs. Clay responds "Yes, yes, they were," in a lamenting lilt.

After a half hour or so, she leaves the room. Rahaman continues to watch the tape for a while, pointing out people and events, but then says he's going to bed. He brings a pen and piece of paper. "Write down your name and number," he says, smiling. "We'll look you up." On his way out the door, he turns and laughs and says, "By the way, friends call me Rock."

Then it's just Ali and me. On the TV, it's early 1964 and he's framed on the left by Jim Jacobs and on the right by Drew "Bundini" Brown. "They both dead now," he says, an acute awareness of his own mortality in his tone.

For a time, he continues to stare at the old Ali on the screen, but eventually he loses interest in peering at distant mountains of his youth. "Did my mom go upstairs? Do you know?" he asks, his voice carrying no farther than mine would if I had my hand over my mouth.

"Yeah, I think she's probably asleep."

He nods, stands, and leaves the room, presumably to check on her. When he comes back he's moving heavily. His shoulder hits the side of the door to the kitchen. He goes in and comes out with two fistfuls of cookies. Crumbs are all over his mouth. He sits beside me on the sofa. Our knees are touching. Usually, when a man gets this close, I pull away. He offers a couple cookies. When he's through eating, he yawns a giant's yawn, closes his eyes, and seems to go dead asleep.

"Champ, you want me to leave?" I say. "Am I keeping you up?"

He slowly opens his eyes and is back to our side of the Great Mystery. The pores on his face suddenly look huge, his features elongated, distorted, like someone's in an El Greco. He rubs his face the way I rub mine when I haven't shaved in a week.

"No, stay," he says. His tone is very gentle.

"You'd let me know if I was staying too late?"

He hesitates slightly before he answers. "I go to bed at eleven," he says.

With the volume turned this low on the TV, you hear the videotape's steady whir. "Can I ask a serious question?" I say. He nods okay.

"Does it bother you that you're a great man not being allowed to be great?"

"Wh-wh-what you mean, 'not allowed to be great'?" he says, his voice hardly finding its way out of his body.

"I mean . . . let me think about what I mean . . . I mean the things you seem to care most about, the things you enjoy doing best, the things the rest of us think of as *being* Muhammad Ali, those are precisely the things that have been taken from you. It just doesn't seem fair."

"You don't question God," he says, his voice rattling in his throat.

"Okay, I respect that, but . . . Aw, man, I don't have any business talking to you about this."

"No, no, go on," he says.

"It just bothers me," I tell him. I'm thinking about the obvious ironies, thinking about Ali continuing to invent, and be invented by, his own mythology. About how he used to talk easier, maybe better, than anybody in the world. (Has anyone in history so liked the sweet and spiky melodies of his own voice?) About how he sometimes still thinks with speed and dazzle, but it often takes serious effort for him to communicate even with people close to him. About how he may have been the world's best athlete— when just walking, he used to move with the grace of a cat turning a corner; now, at night, he stumbles around the house. About how it's his left hand, the same hand from which once slid that great Ali snake-lick of a jab—the most visible phenomenon of his boxing greatness—the very hand with which he won more than 230 fights, it's *his left hand*, not his right, that shakes almost continuously. And I'm thinking how his major source of pride, his "prettiness," remains almost intact. If Ali lost forty pounds, in the right kind of light he would still look classically

Greek. The seeming precision with which things have been excised from Ali's life sort of spooks me.

"I know why this has happened," Ali says. "God is showing me, and showing *you*"—he points his shaking index finger at me and widens his eyes—"that I'm just a man, just like everybody else."

We sit a long quiet time then and watch his flickering image on the television screen. It's now 1971 and there's footage of him training for the first Frazier fight. Our Most Public Figure was then the World's Most Beautiful Man and the Greatest Athlete of All Times, his copper skin glowing under the fluorescents, secret rhythms springing in loose firmness from his fingertips.

"Champ, I think it's time for me to go," I say again, and make an effort to stand.

"No, stay. You my man," he says, and pats my leg. He has always been this way, always wanted to be around people. And I take his accolade as one of the greatest compliments of my life.

"I'll tell you a secret," he says, and leans close. "I'm gowna make a comeback."

"What?" I say. I think he's joking, hope he is, yet something in his tone makes me uncertain. "You're not serious?" I ask.

And suddenly there is power in his voice. "I'm gowna make a comeback," he repeats louder, more firmly.

"Are you serious?"

"The timing is perfect. They'd think it was a miracle, wouldn't they?" He's speaking in a distinct, familiar tone; he's very easy to understand. It's almost the voice I remember from when I met him in 1975. In short, Ali sounds like Ali.

"Wouldn't they?" he asks again.

"It *would* be a miracle," I say.

"Nobody'll take me serious at first. But then I'll get my weight down to two-fifteen and have an exhibition at Yankee Stadium or someplace, then they'll believe. I'll fight for the title. It'll be bigger than the Resurrection." He stands and walks out to the center of the room.

"It'd be good to get your weight down," I say.

"Watch this," he says, and dances to his left, studying himself in the mirror above the TV. His clean white shoes bounce around the carpet; I marvel at how easily he moves. His white clothing accentuates his movements in the dark room; the white appears to make him glow. He starts throwing punches, not the kind he'd tossed at me earlier, but now really letting them go. I'd honestly thought that what he'd thrown in the yard was indicative of what he had left. But what he'd done was allow me to play; he'd wanted me to enjoy myself.

"Look at the TV. That's 1971 and I'm just as fast now." One second, two seconds, twelve punches flash in the night. This can't be real. But apparently it is. The old man can still do it: He can still make fire appear in the air. He looks faster standing in front of me than does the ghostlike Ali image on the screen. I wish I had a video camera to tape this. Nobody would believe me.

"And I'll be even faster when I get my weight down," he tells me.

"You know more now, too," I find myself admitting. What am I saying? And why am I saying this?

"Do you believe?" he asks.

"Well . . ." I say. God, the Parkinson's is affecting his sanity. Look at the gray shining in his hair. The guy can hardly walk, for Christ's sake. Just because he was my boyhood idol doesn't mean I'm blind to what his life is now like.

And Ali throws another three dozen blows at the gods of mortality—he springs a *triple* hook off of a jab, each punch so quick it trails lines of light—drops straight right leads in multiples, explodes into a blur of uppercuts, and the air pops, and his fists and feet whir. This is his best work. His highest art. The very combinations that no one has ever thrown quite like Muhammad Ali. When he was fighting, he typically held back some; this is the stuff he seldom used—or *had* to use.

"Do you believe?" he asks, breathing hard, but not much harder than I would if I'd thrown the number of serious punches he's just thrown.

"They wouldn't let you, even if you could do it," I say, thinking, *There's too much concern everywhere for your health. Everybody thinks they see old Mr. Thanatos waiting for you.*

"Do you *believe*?" he asks again.

"I believe," I hear myself say.

He stops dancing and points a magician's finger at me. Then I get the look, the smile, that has closed one hundred thousand interviews. "April Fools'," he says, and takes his seat beside me again. His mouth is hanging open and he's breathing hard. The smell of sweat comes from his skin.

We sit in silence for several minutes. I look at my watch. It's 11:18. I hadn't realized it was that late. I'd told Lyn I'd be in by eight.

"Champ, I better go home. I have a wife and kids waiting."

"Okay," he says almost inaudibly, and yawns the kind of long uncovered yawn people usually do among family.

He's bone-tired, I'm tired, too, but I want to leave him by saying something that will mean something to him, something that will set me apart from the two billion other people he's met, that will imprint me indelibly in his memory and will make the kind of impact on his life that he has made on mine. I want to say the words that will cure his Parkinson's syndrome.

Instead I say, "See you Easter, Champ."

He coughs and gives me his hand. "Be cool and look out for the ladies." His words are so volumeless that I don't realize what he's said until I'm halfway out the door.

I don't recall picking up the book he signed, but I must have: It's beside my typewriter now. I can't remember walking across his mom's yard and don't remember starting the Volvo. But I do recall what was playing on the tape deck. It was "The Promise of Living" from the orchestral suite to Aaron Copland's *The Tender Land*.

*   *   *

I don't forget Lyn's gallon of milk. The doors to the grocery store whoosh closed behind me. For this time of night, there are quite a few customers in the store. They seem to move more as floating shadows than as people.

I'm not the same; I'm changed. And I know it. An old feeling comes across me that I almost immediately recognize. The sensation is much like going out into the day-to-day world after making love for the first time. It's the same sense of having landed in a lesser reality. And of having a secret that the rest of the world can't see. I'll have to wake Lyn and share the memory of this feeling with her.

I reach to grab the milk jug and catch a reflection of myself in the chrome at the dairy counter. There's a half smile on my face and I hadn't realized it.

Six

On Sunday afternoon, Lyn and our daughter, Johanna, and I drive to Mrs. Clay's; we leave Isaac with a babysitter, not wanting to risk him breaking something or stressing out Ali's mom.

"You should have brought him along," Mrs. Clay says to Lyn as we take seats in the family room. "He couldn't do anything I haven't seen before. When Ali was a baby, I was changing his diaper. I leaned over and he hit me in the mouth. Knocked out two teeth."

Ali stands from his seat on the sofa, walks to Lyn, hugs her (she sheepishly returns his embrace), hugs me, then reaches for Johanna, who quickly scurries behind me and clutches my pants legs. I coax her out and Ali picks her up and cradles her to his chest.

His twin daughters, Rasheeda and Jamillah, students at the University of Illinois, are in town for the

holiday. Ali performs magic for Johanna (who continues to hide behind me at every opportunity) and ar-
gues with his daughters about their style of dress and
makeup. "Christian men'll be lookin' at you," he says,
leaning forward and arching his head with urgency.
"You'll get yourselves in trouble."

Do his daughters recognize that their father is
speaking as much about the Muhammad Ali of the
seventies as he is about "Christian men"? The girls are
tall, lithe, classically beautiful, generally unharmed by
the world. And young enough to believe themselves
to be immortal.

"Daddy, you're so old-fashioned," they tell him in
stereo. Jamillah punches him kind of hard on the left
biceps and from the other side Rasheeda dismisses
him with a peck on the cheek.

We eat pound cake and vanilla ice cream and watch
TV for a while. Lyn and Mrs. Clay talk about the
season. Lyn promises to paint Ali's mom a vase of vi-
olets, daffodils, and buttercups. I ask Ali if he still
travels a lot. "All the time," he says. "Just got back
from Afghanistan. That's where I was when Bundini
died. Flyin' to Kuwait on Tuesday. Be gone a few
days."

As Lyn, Johanna, and I prepare to leave, he asks
Rahaman to give me the phone number at his farm in
Michigan. "Call me," he says. "You my man."

Early Wednesday morning, while driving to the
Lexington stores, I listen to the news. Kuwait Air-
lines Flight 422, on which Ali was a scheduled pas-

senger, has been hijacked. Two people have been murdered and the remainder are hostages. I pull into a rest area and call Mrs. Clay's. She answers the phone. "Don't worry," she says of her (and Allah's) famous son. "He's still here. His trip was canceled yesterday morning."

Seven

When the alarm clock goes off on Thursday, I roll over and look at Lyn. "It's going to be gorgeous today," the radio weatherman says. "Expected high in the upper sixties."

I look at the shadows of beginning wrinkles beside Lyn's eyes, study the vasculature around her temples and in her eyelids, and gently push the tresses back off her forehead. Her hair no longer catches light the way it used to; it's a bit darker and more coarse. And her nose and cheekbones are slightly more prominent than they once were. We're getting on in years.

I slide out of bed and cover her with the blanket, grab a holey T-shirt and the pair of slacks I'd worn the day before, and pull them on, the pager still on my hip. I've gained so much weight since we've been in Louisville that I can hardly button my pants. I go downstairs and open a kitchen cabinet, pull out a cereal bowl with a drawing of a cartoon bear embedded in the plastic, then put it back, deciding I don't want to eat. I close the cabinet and take a seat at the kitchen table. After a while, I look at my watch. It's 8:42. I should've been on my way to Lexington by now.

At the front door, I put on the beat-up sneakers I wear to mow the lawn and step outside to stretch, watching wind in a stand of locust trees across the road and feeling it on my skin. I pick up the morning paper and, after glancing at headlines that seem to have been written for someone else, toss it on top of the stack of other unread papers just inside the door. How is it that people read this junk every day? What good does it do us? How short are our lives and how slowly the mysteries are revealed.

The world is so big and before meeting Ali, I'd been narrowing everything down so much. The sun rises peach-fat over limestone-studded hills. Fog shines fluorescently near the treetops. A freshly dead rabbit is on the road right in front of the house. Sunlight glistens off the animal's exposed remains.

I stand beside the road and watch folks all boxed up behind the wheels of their cars, looking restrained, flat-faced, and empty-eyed on their way to the nine-to-fives. After a while, I turn and walk down to the river, watch mist spiraling from the water, listen to the cawing of a crow in the woods on the other side, pick a few freshwater clams from the sand, and watch and listen to waves lapping against the shore.

"I am way fucking off course," I say aloud, eyeing a big barge of crushed cars as it chugs downstream toward the Mississippi. "This is not the life I want."

I watch the sun dissipate the fog. I stare at the river and the mist and the barge and the trees on the other side until I'm surprised to feel Lyn fold her arms around my waist from behind. I've been surprised several times over the past few days. I turn to face her. "We're still young," I say. "Why have I been carrying myself so old lately?"

She doesn't answer. I guess I didn't expect her to. She's standing barefoot on the wet grass, unclothed save for being wrapped in the blanket. Now that consciousness has flowed back into her face, she looks ineffably beautiful.

"Aren't your feet cold?" I ask, knowing that they have to be; her body, or what I can see of it outside the blanket, is as firm as a trout's, her skin tight and bristling in the way that people get only when they are chilled.

"Sure, but it feels good, too," she says. "Come back in the house and make yourself a cup of tea."

"You know what I'm going to do, don't you?" I ask. She nods and looks concerned.

"Well?" I say.

"I don't see how we can make it," she says, "but maybe I'm wrong. Just get a job when it doesn't work out."

She stands and turns to leave. "Come on back inside," she repeats, still looking worried. "I'll have your tea waiting."

I kick off shoes, feel grass and ground beneath my feet. Of course it's cold, yet Lyn's right: There's pleasure and freedom in the experience, too. I take a breath in deep through nose and mouth and realize that, for the first time in years, it doesn't hurt to breathe. At the very instant of knowing it, I relax even more. Something inside me, something deeper than muscles, harder than a fist, something that has been balled up tight and hard for so long that I had even forgotten I had clenched it . . . it suddenly re-relaxes.

"I don't have to be who you want me to be," Ali had once said, and I had heard him. I had felt that this was true of me, too.

Now I'm thirty-seven years old: It's finally time to prove it.

I pull my watch from my arm and without looking at it, fling it out across the water. It plunks and is gone. Sixty feet deep. I yank the beeper from my hip and before it has the chance to ever beckon me again, I throw it as far as I can. I envision it sinking into the mud of this old, old river. Right beside Cassius Clay's 1960 Olympic gold medal.

Eight

Friday morning, I call the home office and resign. They offer 120 days' severance pay (minus the cost of the beeper). This is far more time than I've ever had without having to work; I'm pretty sure it'll be enough to finally find out if I can write.

I grab a recent issue of *Esquire* from the nightstand, flip to the masthead, pick an editor's name that reminds me of a favorite chocolate treat when I was a kid, go to my study, call New York.

The editor answers his phone. I tell him my name, history, what I want to write, and why. After we talk for probably a half hour, he says, "Here's Lee's extension. Give him a call in about fifteen minutes. I'll go talk with him."

When I reach Lee, I say, "There's nothing pitiful about Ali's life. He's not who people believe him to be. If you're patient and wait on him, he still says and does remarkable things. Sometimes he comes across almost as a seer."

I tell Lee that I want to call the story "My Dinner with Ali." He offers $2,500 for six thousand words. It's the equivalent of about five weeks' salary after taxes. "This is a big opportunity," he says. He gives me two months to write the story; my deadline is June 1.

Nine

To calm myself and prepare for serious work, I take long walks in the woods and down by the river and lock myself in the silence of my study to open myself up to the muse. Although I plan to write a page a day until the story is complete, it quickly develops a life of its own. Every day, when I close the typewriter, I'm surprised by how much has been written and how well it reads. Just as I'd been anticipating meeting Ali for all these years, it's as if the universe has been waiting to write this story.

The writer's life suits me. I rise each morning before the sky goes orange and work a couple hours until everyone else wakes. After breakfast, I drive Johanna to school and return home. It's downright sanctifying not to have to shave every day or to put on somebody else's idea of work clothes; I usually wear gym shorts, and sometimes a T-shirt, as I write.

For the first time since I quit kickboxing, I have time to comfortably attend to things other than a job. I eat better—mountains of fresh Asian-style vegetables: crisp, thick broccoli stalks, razor-lean carrot slices, bamboo shoots, water chestnuts, bok choy, brown rice. Lyn cooks American Southern, too: pintos and squash and limas and black-eyed peas and cornbread, their fragrances swirling, rising, filling the air, smelling at once of earth and of sky.

I start working out again and, as I did in my youth, see physical training as a personal purification ritual. Following the path of the river, I run a couple miles a day, weaving in and out of the woods, throwing punches and kicks at branches and leaves. I grind out a few nightly sets of push-ups and some abdominal work, too, and within a few days, I begin an indoor workout. My office doubles as a sweat lodge; I start with three rounds of shadowboxing and a couple with the jump rope. I've almost forgotten how hard it can be to swing a strand of cow's hide and hop up and down for a while. With the fat jiggling on my hips, I feel like an aging bullfrog with a feather hanging out of his mouth, trying to fly. Pretty soon, though, I no longer pink-stripe my calves with the rope and I jump with a stutter step, one foot in front of the other. I jump toe first, too, then heel first; step cross-legged across the floor; even whip the rope beneath my feet two turns for every time I jump. I envision gaining strength as I jump, not losing it. At first I'm tight and stiff. But soon it comes. My body loosens, opens, lets go, begins to hum. It feels righteous to train not to punch or kick anyone in the head and body, and not to become a world-class athlete, but simply for the beauty of the movement.

Within two weeks, I'm up to five rounds of shadow and four with the rope, using my fear of the future to push me on. Where, as a kid, I had trained to Marvin Gaye, Stevie Wonder, and James Brown, I now develop my workouts around a couple songs by Pat Metheny from his *First Circle* CD; several complex, edgy, yet lyrical, untamable, and enigmatic Celtic battle tunes; all the cosmic cowboy newgrass I can find by Jerry Douglas and by Béla Fleck; and excerpts from Aaron Copland's *Billy the Kid* and the opening to *Lincoln Portrait*, both of which sound something like what Copland might've written had he been commissioned to score a work about Ali. I cool down to some fairly plaintive Celtic melodies and Vaughan Williams pastorals. The final cut on my workout tape, the one favorite from the old days, is Van Morrison's "Into the Mystic."

Although I develop shinsplints from all the running and jumping (God, these ache way too much to be shinsplints, I think, until I realize, oops, I'm thirty-seven years old; these are *middle-aged* shinsplints), my energy level increases, I'm more attentive and watchful, ideas flow—even though I'm scared out of my pond about where my life is headed.

About two weeks into the writing, the typewriter screws up big-time: When I press the space bar, it won't type the next key I hit. I have to backspace, then poke the letter again. This not only dramatically slows the process, it disrupts thought patterns, keeps me from thinking, stifles the flow. Maybe this is a little like Ali's speech problem. For him, trying to talk in regular sentences must be similar to writing a story with a worn ink ribbon and keys that don't work right. Words fade and the Tao is blocked. It's remarkable that he seems not to get frustrated.

Each night in bed, Lyn reads what I've written. "It's good," she says, "but I don't know . . . I have bad feelings—I just don't know if they'll publish it."

The accuracy of Lyn's intuitiveness has long before been proved and I usually listen seriously to what she says she feels. But I'm pretty good at visiting my instincts, too (or maybe they're pretty good at visiting me). And this time I have to go with what's in my gut.

I tell her that I think she's nuts; it's too damned good not to run. "I will be the Greatest Writer of All Times," I say, but I'm more nostalgic than serious; I make the statement with a doggish grin and a wink.

I finish a rough draft in three weeks and spend another four days polishing it and being sure I've said everything I want to say as well as I can say it. On

May 1, I swear it vibrates in my hands as I read it one last time. I drive to the post office and drop it in the box, sending it on its way to New York a full month early.

Ten

The next week, as I wait to hear from *Esquire*, I construct my first-ever résumé (Ali studies, kickboxing, and video store experience don't go far in corporate America) and read the "Help Wanted" section of the Louisville *Courier-Journal*, circling several sales jobs, each of which looks almost as tempting as a one-way ticket to Riker's Island.

In the month since I've met Ali and he gave me his phone number, I haven't called, not wanting to bother him, and feeling sort of intrusive simply for having the number. After all, it's not like I'm a close friend; hundreds of thousands of folks (this isn't an overstatement) have known Ali better than I. And as he himself admits, his kindness has been abused in hundreds of ways by untold legions.

Wednesday, I haven't heard back from my editor

and I'm so nervous that I'm looking for anything to keep me busy. So I tromp down to the basement, root through the stuff we never unpacked after the move from North Carolina, and find two big boxes of Ali newspapers and magazines that I've carried with me as I've moved from place to place, eleven times in ten years. I lug the boxes upstairs and sort through every yellowed, musty item: hundreds of articles that date from December 1963 through the present. Going through these stories and looking at the old photos, I can't help but consider how the young Ali's seemingly endless energy had promised that he would never get old. And how in many ways he is now older than just about anyone his age.

Yet I don't feel bad for him. Muhammad Ali is not the first artist to have suffered for, or because of, his art and beliefs. One of the first things you notice when spending time with him is how quickly you forget about his malady. Ali doesn't act handicapped in any way; we therefore quickly understand that he is not. Ali's life is still more interesting than about anyone else's. He seems less than fulfilled only when we consider him in the smallest of ways, when we don't recognize that his affliction and its aura of silence enlarges his legend and his life. Most of the writing (and the talk) about Ali, not only now (about his health) but over the decades, has served to inaccurately limit him, to minimize him and his existence.

I don't have to be who you want me to be. One of the major themes of Ali's life is that he doesn't fall into our limited notions of who he is, can't be accurately capsulized. His life and spirit ooze out of the sides of the carton.

Sifting through these boxes of decay, I put aside no more than ten items I care about—the program and ticket stubs from when Lyn and I tried to get married at the Shavers fight, a few posters and magazines, a copy of the classic 1970 Ken Regan head shot in which jeweled planets of sweat ride Ali's countenance like cold water poured on a hot copper frying-pan sky.

I carefully lay the small bundle in my bottom desk drawer, reseal the boxes, and call Rahaman to ask if I can stop by for a few minutes.

At Mrs. Clay's, Rock comes out to the car and helps carry the two heavy boxes up to the house. Sitting on the sofa, I show him a few items: newspaper and magazine pieces about the Liston fights, Ali's conversion to Islam, the arrest for draft evasion, the epic first battle with Frazier, the Supreme Court overturning the draft conviction, Foreman being voodooed by Ali in Zaire, the Thrilla in Manila, the boxing lesson he gave Spinks in their second contest, a recent story about Ali saving a suicidal man who intended to leap from a window ledge of a Los Angeles skyscraper. "Jump! Jump!" the crowd chanted as Ali was passing on the street. Ali went to the man, leaned out the window, talked the man in by promising to help him. He bought the man clothes, gave him money, helped him get therapy, found him a job. Rahaman asks if an enlargement can be made of a

Newsweek photo of Ali, himself, and their father with Gerald Ford at the White House. I tell him I'll see what I can do.

"Never seen a collection like this," Rock says. "Nothin' this big."

He gets up from the sofa and walks to a closet, coming back with a long cardboard tube. "These are my paintings," he says, popping a metal seal from the end of the tube. "Pictures of my brother."

He unrolls canvas after canvas, most crumbling with age and abuse, some water-damaged, a few in top condition. He has a strong sense of color and form, and I tell him so.

"Ain't nothin' compared to my daddy," he says.

I say that I've heard his father is a real painter.

"Aw, man, he paints *beauuuu*-tiful," Rahaman says, stretching the "U" sound like a giant rubber band. "*Beauuuu*-tiful," he repeats, leaning his head skyward as if speaking to an audience in the clouds. "I'll never be nothin' compared to Cash."

I tell Rock that I need to head home. "Let me help with your boxes," he says.

"They're yours now," I say. "I wanted to give them to someone who'd take care of them. Too bad there's no museum to donate them to."

"Maybe there's gonna be," Rahaman says. "A fella's tryin' to start a boxin' museum in Louisville. Ali'll be in town this weekend to help him out. We're all gonna meet at a gym downtown. Why don't you come?"

*   *   *

Saturday afternoon around one-thirty, armed only with a street number and a general idea of the building's whereabouts, I drive past a couple times, first overlooking it, then saying "Nah, that can't be it," but, maybe, that tiny little box over there, over there near the river and nothing else except some abandoned warehouses with shattered windows and a few wind-whipped scrub pines, that run-down shack over there with the rutted dirt parking area and the fish market behind it, maybe that's the gym. Yes, it is! The third time by, a black Cadillac limo pulls into the parking lot and Ali's father, Cassius Marcellus Clay, Sr., steps out.

There's only one sign on the crumbling concrete block building: a swinging, creaking, rusted metal Royal Crown Cola advertisement that at one time had been red, white, and blue. The windows have been covered with sheets of plywood. Neon green spray paint to the left of the door reads "Boo! Scary Spook Place." If Ali saw this upon entering, surely he had some fun with it. I imagine him putting on an openmouthed grimace. "Spook? I'll show ya a scary spook!" he would shout.

The first thing I notice upon opening the door is that the long, garishly lit room smells ripe, slick, and sweet with worn leather, old sweat, and oft-used liniments. In the right corner, there's a small, abused, blue-roped ring, its large-pored, once-bleached canvas colored by body salts, blood, and Atomic Balm. Near the rear of the room is a heavy bag, its thick black leather cover split and nearly ripped from its body. Sinners have certainly left this bag enlightened.

Today, though, this building is not a temple of the body, not the abode of mad warrior monks at communion with the gods of violence; the mood today is festive, up-front celebratory: Red, yellow, blue, and orange balloons hang from the ring's corner posts; crepe paper has been strung throughout the gym; three sliced watermelons and a punch bowl filled with a thick pink fruit drink are on a long card table near the center of the floor. There are about seventy-five noisy people present—men, women, children—some dressed in Sunday best, others in T-shirts and jeans. An eight-millimeter movie projector to the left of the ring is clacking and spinning, throwing sepia-tinted images onto a blank area of the crumbling plaster wall: films of the teenage Cassius Clay jumping rope and blistering a heavy bag and a speed bag.

A couple ancient boxing trainers are sitting on straw-backed wooden chairs beside the projector, one at each corner, rooted, gnarled, mysterious, and self-contained as bonsai trees. Ali's boyhood friend and former heavyweight champion Jimmy Ellis is standing to the right of the ring and beside one of the trainers, his big hand tender on the old man's shoulder. Ellis wears dark glasses these days, having been blinded in the left eye in a final fight.

Ali's father has taken a spot next to Ellis. At five-foot-ten or so, Cassius Clay looks like a miniature, much less benign, version of Rahaman. In his youth, Cash had a darkly handsome rascality about him; in his seventies, he is bent, razor-thin, and his eyes are clouded. Cash is crooning "For the Good Times" in a Vegas-fake-wise voice that sounds of dusk and spent charcoal, performing for anyone who'll listen; at this moment, it's for a tall grinning white man who looks like a game show host or a politician and who's being led around the room by a camcorder.

Ali is sitting on a folding metal chair beside Cash, appearing to ignore his father and looking as distracted as a ninth grader in algebra class on the day before spring break. Rahaman is to Ali's right, holding a clear plastic cup of punch and sporting a grin as big and goofy as the guy's with the camcorder—Rahaman's face intrinsically different, of course, in that it harbors none of that cracker's gleaming old Southern "Can-you-believe-what-these-crazy-niggers-are-doin'?" malice about it.

"This is borin'," Ali suddenly yells, and stands, immediately commanding the attention of most everyone in the room. He's dressed as some sort of emissary, in a manner beyond fashion, with quiet, near-timeless elegance: custom-tailored blue pinstripe suit, lightly starched white shirt, royal red patterned silk tie, polished black leather uppers. For his entire public life, even Ali's haircut has transcended fashion: It's neither short or long; it perfectly halos his features; as long as there are haircuts, it will be considered stylish.

Ali steps up to the person nearest him, a burly, red-bearded, tough-acting country gent in a Hawaiian shirt. "Did you call me a niggah?" he yells.

The recipient of the accusation jumps back, startled and scared, then embarrassedly laughs. "Just joshin'," Ali says, looking sheepish and very young. He offers the man his hand, then whirls away, searching for the next soul to incite and cajole.

Within seconds, he's playfully winging clownish punches at several people near him. Although he's in play mode, his moves come fairly loose and reasonably fast.

"Did you used to box?" he whispers respectfully to a middle-aged midget who's wearing sunglasses and a black baseball cap with red stitching that reads ELVIS FOREVER.

Dozens of people take turns trading shots with Ali. He pretends to get knocked down by an eighty-pound girl who's wearing a pair of gold pillow-sized boxing gloves that Ali has just autographed for her. As he rises from the floor, he turns and recognizes me and, after presenting the girl with a kiss on the cheek, walks over and gives me his hand. "Didn't know you'd be here," he says, his tone determinedly innocent. "You surprise me."

It's me who's surprised. With Ellis, his dad, Rahaman, the old trainers, and so many people in the room with whom he seems to share history, I'm stunned he even knows who I am, much less that he pays any attention to me. "I wanted to see you," I say.

Like in his yard the day we met, he motions to me with his eyes and puts his hands beside his head. I dance to my left in exactly the style I learned from him twenty-five years before.

"You found a live one," somebody yells to Ali.

"I could be your daddy," Ali says to me, "if I was white."

Ali and I slip and move around the old wooden floor for probably forty-five seconds. Like before, he seems a little surprised by my speed and style. As he tries to fire at me, I beat him to the punch. "You don't like black folks, do you?" he shouts. I find myself smiling. I feel good.

He points at a big blond adolescent, a heavyweight, who's wearing a green polo shirt and who looks like a fraternity kid. The boy comes over and asks advice: "What's the best way to find a manager?" he says. "What do I need to do to go pro?"

Ali's answer is to pump a jab toward the kid's chin. The boy is put off only for a moment. Ali throws a second punch, then waves the kid in with both hands. The boy hesitates a moment, then launches slow, careful punches and slips mechanically, but nicely, as Ali throws back.

"Do the shuffle, Champ," I shout. For two seconds, he is once again hidden rhythm's dancer: His shiny street dogs blur into his own private dance step.

After about thirty seconds of moving around with the college kid, Ali motions toward the ring and removes his jacket. I'm sure he must be joking, but he picks up a pair of licorice-colored Everlasts and walks to the ring apron.

As he steps between the ropes, he pulls his tie from his neck and the sixteen-ounce sheaths of leather are quickly strapped on his wrists. "Gowna do five rounds," he yells to the people gathering ringside. The volume level in his voice has greatly increased. And the sound no longer issues from high in his throat; there's a roundness to his words.

"Gowna teach you what it's all about," he says to his smiling opponent, then turns his back and can't suppress a smile himself.

In his corner, the big grinning cracker with the camcorder pulls Ali's shirttail from his trousers; the top button remains fastened. Someone somewhere shouts "Ding," and then it's actually happening—for conceivably the last time ever, sick old Muhammad Ali is really boxing.

A slow-moving cockroach of sweat crawls fat down the small of my back. Although in some ways I don't want to watch and feel almost ashamed to be a witness, I ache to know if he can still really do it.

For the first thirty seconds, I want to wince with each blow thrown. Ali doesn't seem able to get on his toes; his balance doesn't look good. He regularly slings quick-seeming jabs, but every punch misses. I believe the frat kid may be holding back in order to avoid hurting our ailing legend.

Suddenly, around one minute into the round, the Champ drops his gloves to his sides, exposing his chin, and when his opponent tries to reach him with punches, he pulls his head back and away, just like the Ali we remember, causing the kid to miss by less than an inch. I hear myself say "Ooh," and find that I almost immediately relax some.

At the beginning of Round Two, Ali's face is animated, centered, serious. "No excuses," he says to himself.

The kid comes out hard, apparently wanting to make it a real fight. He thumps Ali with stiff punches to the chin and to the chest. Ali covers up. "Keep movin'," he says, "keep punchin'."

The college kid steps in to throw another shot and Ali stabs him with a perfectly timed counter jab that's sweet as a bite from the last tangy apple of autumn. The kid's head is turned ninety degrees by the force of the blow. It's a very subtle technique; the punch was not thrown for audience reaction; almost no one in the room recognizes that the kid has been stunned. Fifteen seconds later, Ali shivers the kid's legs with a straight right lead. "Don't hurt him, Champ," Rahaman yells, but there's no need: Ali has backed off.

The kid gets on his bicycle; for a few moments he wears the expression of someone who has just been made aware of his own mortality. Ali continues to box the rest of the round at a level slightly above the boy's abilities (although the boy himself may not recognize it). With twenty seconds left, he zings in a series of eight jabs and a razor of a right, all designed to make only surface contact, but to confirm that he is still Ali.

The old master does three more rounds with less capable students than the frat kid (chasing a rotund guy who's wearing glasses around the ring, spanking him on the seat of his workout pants instead of punching his face or his jiggling body), then he steps awkwardly from the ring and immediately begins to walk his great-granddaddy walk.

I take a seat with him on the apron. "H-h-how did I look?" he asks. He has to repeat the question twice before I understand. Why would he ask *me*? I can't help but wonder. Both of his arms are shaking, as is his head. "D-d-did I surprise you?"

Once more, I admit that he did. He chuckles and nods, satisfied to have kept the world in orbit.

He trudges over to the refreshment table, looking for something to drink. The punch is gone. He pulls a chunk of watermelon from the rind, juice dripping between his fingers, stuffs it in his mouth, picks up the entire melon, turns it on its side, and lets juice slowly drip into a cup, which he expeditiously drains.

He tugs on his jacket and, in front of a big mirror that's used for shadowboxing, takes probably five minutes to convince his fingers to knot his tie, showing no impatience. We walk from the gym into a thin mist. The sidewalk is empty. A wet and shining blue Chevy pickup with a camper attached to the bed is at the curb. An older black gentleman wearing a straw hat and holding an umbrella is leaning against the truck. Ali walks to the Chevy stiffly, silently, and with great dignity. He has a little trouble getting into his seat on the passenger's side. I close his door. He waves to me.

"Be cool," he says. I wait for the rest of his catchphrase. But he surprises me once again. "Remain wise," he says.

With a trail of blue smoke shining in the air, the

pickup pulls from the curb. The last thing I notice, as the truck disappears in the drizzle, is the brand name painted in huge white letters on the camper's rear window. The letters read BRAHMA.

SECTION II

Into the Mystic

Eleven

Sunday morning, July 16. A foghorn blows, tugging me from sleep, and I listen to a barge churn upstream toward Cincinnati. Lyn's downstairs; the coffee smell is thick and pots are clanking. I lie in bed, feeling sun on my skin, considering the arc of my life and feeling more connected than I remember having felt or, more precisely, feeling more aware of the connectedness.

As a kid, I had wanted to belong. And now I know that I do, and that I have all along. How could it have been otherwise, how could it ever be otherwise for anyone?

Interconnectedness. All those years past, if I hadn't been convinced that writing was the very thing for me, if I hadn't been almost desperate in that ambition, if I'd gotten a full-time job, Lyn wouldn't've left and I wouldn't've moved back to Winston-Salem and managed a store for the only video chain in the country that could've transferred me from North Carolina to Louisville. And, of course, I would not have met Ali—and met him in a way that felt so . . . well, inevitable. (Not to mention all the stuff about my mom's death and stunting my growth and being the littlest kid in school and obsessed with fighting and all that.)

Inevitability. If Ali hadn't been a boxer, and if he hadn't been the best ever at what he did, if he hadn't felt a need to do something of lasting importance, something that would secure for him a place in history, his career would not have lasted nearly so long—unfortunately against the best-ever generation of heavyweights—and his health and his life would now be . . . well, you see: He would not be Ali the mystic, Ali the whispering muse. The connections seem no less profound than to be serendipitous.

But then, is Ali the mystic, or am I?

It is, after all, the writer's journey to bathe in dreams and in wind and in lightning. Or at least it has been a big part of the trip for this aspiring writer. Am I projecting my vision, and who I am, onto Ali?

"You'll see what your eyes will allow you to see," Ali had told Joe Frazier all those years before.

In his statement I had heard the implied possibility of transcendence, of a life beyond the mundane—as well as the thesis that the ordinary was not mundane at all, depending, perhaps, on how it is viewed.

Maybe there are mystics everywhere. Many sixties and seventies kids (of which Ali was one and I another) have been hunching the mysteries for years. Indeed, swimming in ether is much of what those decades were about for many of us. In the years since, we have celebrated the mystic in the music we listen to, the clothes we wear, the food we eat, the art we choose, the books we read. When seen this way, ours is a generation of mystics.

Yet it's tough to balance such ruminative magic against this morning's realities. While I've been in bed thinking near-rapturous thoughts, Isaac has been crying. Every couple minutes his volume has ebbed and I've believed he's about to stop, then he cranks up again, shaking the air and sounding pretty forlorn.

Maybe the heat's bothering him. Surely it can't be helping. This has been the hottest summer on record. Nearly every day for over a month, the highs have been ninety-five or more. We haven't had a drop of rain since early May and it feels like we might never see clouds again. Ponds and lakes are drying up and the river is at a fifty-year low. The morning air, typically cool and soothing this time of year, feels heavier and more ominous with each day.

I wish I could say that the weather is the only oppressive thing in our lives. Tuesday afternoon two weeks ago, I had a second interview for a sales position with a big pharmaceutical firm. I was pretty interested in the job (it paid good money and I'd be issued a company car) until the district manager, a big blond otherwise pleasant fellow in his mid-forties, smilingly told me that if I took the position, I wouldn't be allowed to write *and* I'd have to sign a contract guaranteeing that any future writing income would be turned over to the company. Un-fucking-real. And right when I got home from this disappointment, there was a call from a vice president of the video chain; he said that my next weekly severance check would be my last. I told him that I'd been promised four months' pay.

"We've decided we can't keep you on that long," he said. "Cash flow's tight."

"Can you give me one more week?" I asked.

"We'll let you know."

That Thursday, the check arrived right on time in the mail. The following week, there was nothing. First thing last Monday, I drove downtown to apply for unemployment and after waiting in lines and filling out forms for half a day, I found out that I qualified to get $167 a week for ninety days. And that we'll probably have to wait about three weeks to receive the first check. While I was out, Daddy had left a message.

"I stopped by one of the stores to rent a movie," came his voice from the answering machine. "Told the guy at the counter that my son works for Video Village in Kentucky. He asked your name. When I told him, he said he heard you didn't work there no more. Come on, Dave—what's goin' on? I just about had me a heart attack right there on the spot."

I should've told Daddy before now. I wish I had. But he worries so much. All during the years I kick-boxed (when I was trying to become four-limbed lightning), and then when I was working to teach

myself to write (to become left-minded thunder), he
worried that I'd never grow up. Ever since I got promoted to district manager, although Daddy tries
never to show anything resembling emotion, it's not
been hard to tell how big-time proud he has been.

As soon as I played his message, I called him back
at work and told him just about everything, including
the stuff about meeting Ali and the *Esquire* assignment. "They're paying twenty-five hundred for the
story," I said.

"Twenty-five hundred dollars ain't shit," he said.
Daddy seldom curses. "But you're a full-growed man,
Dave. I can't tell you what to do."

He asked how much we owed in bills for the
month. I told him we needed about a thousand dollars. "We'll come up with it," I said. "*Esquire*'ll pay."

On Wednesday, a note came in the mail. "Dave,
Enclosed is a check for $1,150," it read. "This is the
Balance of the money from the Mutual Fund I had
for you and your Sister using your Mother's Life Ins.
check. Son Please use it to pay your house payment
and the car. With any luck at all this should carry you
over the hump. Please Now don't use this for anything else so I Won't Worry."

Sometimes, considering the money Daddy makes,
it's tough to understand how he's done such a fine job
of taking care of his family for more than forty years.
Life insurance check? No way. Aunts and uncles have
told me that the insurance company didn't make good
on my mother's policy, since it had been taken out
only a few months before she passed.

I deposited Daddy's check, swearing to myself that I'll pay him back out of the *Esquire* money. Including Daddy's money, Lyn and I have less than two thousand dollars in the world. If that runs out, I have no idea how we'll make the mortgage payment. Then there's the big cooling bills from this godawful heat. Man, I wish that *Esquire* would come on through. They could at least send the five hundred they promised for expenses. It's been more than two months since I mailed "My Dinner with Ali" and I still haven't heard from my editor. If he'd just come through with my twenty-five hundred, I could call Daddy and give him some good news with the bad. Although I remain optimistic (Lyn has regularly accused me over the years of being some weird hopeless kind of optimist), I can't afford to sit on my haunches and wait. I've got to find some work real soon. Since Daddy called, although we'd hate to move, Lyn and I've been talking about going back to North Carolina to look for jobs.

It's strange: When I'd been working so many hours in the stores, I longed to spend time outdoors in our miraculous-seeming neighborhood. This summer has just about cured me of that. It's gotten to where I can hardly stand to look out the windows. In the mornings, as I've gone for runs or to apply for jobs, our grass has been so dry that when I've stepped on it, it has made a crunching noise and has crumbled to powder. The meadows are no better off and neither are the pastures on the area horse farms. Every day, the light has been tawny, there's no wind, and the air

smells and feels old; the sky stays yellow all day and
hangs low with smoke from the city. TV weathermen
are calling this the Great Drought of 1989; National
Public Radio is featuring lots of stories about global
warming. Global warming—there's another, hardly
reassuring, study in interconnectedness.

Now the back door slams, jerking me again from
my thoughts. "Get away from me and leave me
alone," Johanna screams at Dallas, our big old snorty
dog, a Dalmatian–English bull mix—we call him a
Damnation.

"Breakfast is ready," Lyn shouts, trying, unsuccess-
fully, not to be exasperated and sounding as if no one
could possibly be listening to her.

By the time I place both feet on the floor, Isaac is
wailing dramatically. I hustle down to his room. He's
sitting up in bed, reddish blond hair sweaty and sticking out at various sharp, seemingly unrelated angles.
His room has a warm, too-sweet odor, the smell of an
old movie house. Beneath him, the sheet of plastic on
his mattress makes a crinkling sound. He's crimson-
faced, his skin's splotchy, and his nose is running into
his mouth. The little guy's in real everyday misery.
When he wakes in one of these states, he's effectively
inconsolable and Lyn usually worries that he's con-
tracted some disease that will kill him or that he was
born with a fatal gene that has decided to reveal itself
on this very morning. Christ, it's hard to live in the
world. It's hard for all of us, no matter who we are, no
matter where or when.

On the way to the kitchen with fresh-diapered,

weepy Isaac hooked in my left arm, I open the door to bring in the paper. I'm in pretty good shape from more than three months' hard training (in addition to everything else I've been doing, I've mounted my old heavy bag in the study beside the desk and I thump it real crisp and pretty for six to eight rounds each day), but the wall of raw heat just about stops me at the threshold; my arms go heavy, my legs feel as if they're about to melt out from under me.

Instead of tossing the *Courier-Journal* on the floor with the other unopened papers as I usually do, I drop it at my place at the table, then pull Isaac's high chair over close and buckle my resisting son into his seat. Lyn takes her chair on the other side of Isaac and next to Johanna, and Dallas plops his drooly self between Johanna and me.

Looking for solace from the heat in my glass of juice, I down it in one sweet gulp. I'm about to fold the first bite of waffle into my mouth when, after scanning headlines at the top of the paper, I flip to the inside sections. And there it is. Right there. Right in front of my face.

I stare for a long disbelieving time. The headline reads:

THE LIGHT THAT SHONE SO BRIGHT
IS NOW A WARM GENTLE GLOW

Somebody surely worked overtime to come up with a header as bad as that.

"What's wrong?" Lyn says. "You look as if a ghost just walked in the room."

"I can't believe it," I say slowly. The back of my neck suddenly throbs. "Maybe he won't see it," I say. "Maybe nobody'll see it. Maybe it's not being run in New York."

There's a tightness in my upper chest; it hurts to breathe. "I just can't believe it," I repeat, chuckling at the irony.

The story takes up the top half of the first page of the Features section and almost a whole inside page. There's a fairly nice watercolor illustration under the headline and on the inside a photo of Ali with, as the caption reads, "his fourth wife, Lonnie, the former Yolanda Williams, at their wedding ceremony in November 1986." Before this morning I would've never believed I could be upset to find a big positive Ali article in my morning paper.

And then I spot the worst of it. Right under the illustration. Small block letters that read *NEW YORK TIMES* NEWS SERVICE.

I fret all day Sunday, keeping Lyn and the kids (and myself) even more miserable than our money worries and the heat would've made us. Monday is Johanna's eighth birthday. I wake early and try to think about enjoying the day with her, try to focus on the little birthday party we're going to have this afternoon at the pool. Instead, I find myself watching the clock until it feels like the appropriate time to call my editor. I leave a message for him, then another.

On Wednesday, when his assistant tells him I'm on the line, he almost immediately picks up his phone and greets me by saying, "It's not nearly as powerful as your story."

I laugh at his New York abruptness. "I don't think so, either," I say.

"But there are similarities," he says. "Both pieces suggest that Ali's health is better than people think."

"I don't know if that's what I'm saying," I tell him. "His health and his life are different than anyone has written. And different from what people expect who've read those stories."

"The *Times* article is all blue sky and daisies," he agrees. "Reads like a TV script. Yours is much more powerful."

I tell him that I'm glad he likes the story, breathing a little better than I have since I mailed it.

"We planned to use it in a special issue next June," he says. "We thought it might be our cover piece."

I don't like the way he's speaking in the past tense, as if "My Dinner with Ali" is ancient, buried history. "Look," I say, "I don't know what to do now. Where do we go from here? Should I rewrite?"

"I'm not Lee and he brought the *Times* story to me. Lee will make the decision."

"If he wants, I'll be pleased to rewrite. There's a lot more I want to say. I keep seeing Ali. Hey, listen . . . why don't I try to get some time with him at his farm in Michigan? Time with Ali is loaded—everything feels weighty, important. He's sort of a walking metaphor. Or maybe he's more like a haiku, a vessel of momentary enlightenment. Visiting with Ali is like church is supposed to be."

"That's probably not a bad idea," my editor says. "I like that idea. Send a letter telling us how you'd rewrite. I'll take it to Lee."

I ask when I'll be paid for my work. We need the money, I tell him. "We'll pay when the story's been officially accepted," I'm told.

By the time we hang up, even with all those mixed messages, I feel fairly untethered, believing I'll soon see Ali again, and convinced that a piece of writing as lovely and skillful as "My Dinner with Ali" just has to be published.

Twelve

Wednesday, July 26. "My man," Ali says, drawing a deep breath to make his voice strong and audible. "Glad to hear from you."

It's the first time I've spoken to him on the phone. I think I'm adjusting to his voice. I say that I've lost my job, money's tight, and that I'm writing a story about him for a magazine and that I think he'll like it. And then I tell him that Lyn and the kids and I might move back to North Carolina. But before we do, I say, I'd like to see him again.

"Be here a few days," he says, and coughs his wet cough. "Come on up."

"What if I bring Rahaman with me? You want me to bring your brother?"

"Don't matter. Come on," he says.

Thirteen

A white seventies convertible Cadillac I haven't seen before is parked under the redwood deck behind the house. The plastic rear window has several fist-sized holes in it.

"Partner," Rahaman says as he lets me in the front, grinning and laughing and reaching to hug me. I haven't seen Rock when he isn't grinning. "Ready to go? Let me get my stuff."

A frayed tan canvas workout bag is at the bottom of the steps. Offering to help, I follow Rock downstairs. As I round the corner, I'm a little startled to find old Cassius Clay, Sr., slouched in the center of the floor with a couple bored-looking, dirty-faced white kids and their father, who's no less scruffy. Cash's balance isn't good; as he turns to watch me enter the room, he rocks back on his heels.

In the ten or so times I've visited, this is the first time Cash has been here. I consider asking after Mrs. Clay, who's nowhere to be seen, but then think better of it. Cash and Mrs. Clay haven't lived in the same house for years. I figure that when they broke up, Ali bought houses for both parents.

Rock asks if I've met his father, then introduces me. "Have you heard my father sing, have you heard Cash sing?" he says. "My father can really sing. He's got a big voice, like Billy Eckstine."

On cue, Cash falls into "Rainy Night in Georgia," making oversized waving gestures with his arms, tilting his head at a slightly elevated angle, and gazing wet-eyed and with stylized profundity into the near distance. "Don't you think my father can sing?" Rahaman asks, softly clapping a large hand on my shoulder. "Can't he sing *goooood*?"

For no apparent reason, Cash abruptly stops crooning and begins to preach in a raspy voice.

"Told him to quit boxin'," he shouts, his yellowed eyes wide and wild and a little glazed. "Shoulda made movies. He was bigger than anybody. Prettier, too, and smarter. I met Elvis—all pimply-faced, ugly next to Ali. Not smart, either."

As Ali's gentleness and pecan beauty were inherited from his mother, ash-black Cash endowed his eldest son with a crazed brilliance, an anxious ambition, and an almost boundless need to be on-stage. Now Cash discontinues his sermon and spins into "For the Good Times," belting out two full verses of the song. Though Rahaman is standing right beside me and I'm looking straight ahead and can't see him, I feel him grinning at his daddy, Cassius Marcellus Clay, that proud, high-styling, regally named painter and singer who, despite ambition and talent, surely stood no real chance of making it among the gentrified Louisville crackerdom of the 1930s and 1940s.

"He's so *goooood*. Ain't my daddy *goooood*?" the younger brother of the world's most famous man asks once again.

According to Rock and to the gas station map, it's a full day's drive from Louisville to the Ali farm in Berrien Springs, near the foot of Lake Michigan and maybe seventy-five miles south of Chicago. We stop to eat fast-food chicken and for Rock to buy grape sodas (I packed a thermos of iced jasmine tea from which I drink cup after cup), but otherwise drive straight through, listening to Aretha and Marvin Gaye tapes, which I brought because Ali likes them and I guess Rock must, too.

It's the first time I've seen the Midwest and as Rock sleeps and snores I try to take in everything on both sides of the road, even if the drought has just about ruined the view. We drive past mile after mile of yellowed, barren soybean plants and brown three-foot-high corn. Through Indiana and into southern Michigan, I watch dust-gray, long, flat fields, shriveled and dying cattails in dry ditches, and geese leaving early on their flyways, wanting/needing/hoping, I guess, to get the fuck away from this near-apocalyptic heat and dryness. Leaves have gone yellow about two months early and have fallen from ghost-barked white birch and sycamores. Rock wakes as we slow for the village of Ganges, Michigan. We stop at the town's one stoplight. Even with marvelous Marvin Gaye's sweet, melting-butter voice pouring reassuringly from the rear speakers, I feel pretty upset about everything I've been watching, pretty depressed by it all.

"Man, we're screwin' up the world so bad," I say, talking to myself as much as to Rock. "I'm worried that it's about too late—that we've done just about enough to destroy it."

To our left, a couple scrawny chickens flap and strut across a gray dirt driveway and through a yard, kicking up dust that seems not to settle but to hang suspended in the windless heat.

"Man, you crazy," Rahaman says. "What you talkin' 'bout, 'we gonna destroy the world.' Man cain't do that. Only Allah can destroy the world."

Even way out here, away from the big cities like Louisville and Indianapolis and Chicago, there's an orange haze everywhere. Soon, a few silver hills rise in the distance on both sides of the road, then the hills are closer to the car and it's still so hot that even running the air conditioner flat out doesn't much help. We drive beside a shallow rocky river, where I turn off the fan, roll down my window, slow the car, listen to the sound of tumbling water, and pretend that the air is moist and cool. There's a little chloro-phyll left in the river reeds and cattails, and bare yellow limbs of willows look wet as if with ice, which helps my fantasy along a bit. On the right, a green metal sign reads VILLAGE OF BERRIEN SPRINGS, HOME OF MARIAH NATASHA BELL, MISS BLOSSOM-TIME 1989. To our left, there's a dam with a wooden waterwheel. We cross a bridge over the river, climb a steep short hill, and enter the township.

Berrien Springs is the size place that once you've driven through it, you might not know everything in town, but you sure won't get lost. Rahaman tells me to make a left at a stoplight at the top of the hill. After a short distance he says, "Go left again, across from the Starlite." For some reason, he thinks that's funny. He grins as if apologizing and laughs and laughs.

We turn where a sign that says STARLITE fronts an otherwise empty field, then go maybe five miles down an unlined tar and gravel road through a neighborhood of small one-story 1950s and 1960s ranch-style houses, at the end of which are two stone pillars, an open wrought-iron gate, and a big white sign with large gilded letters. MUHAMMAD ALI FARMS, the sign reads.

We move slowly through the gate and down a long driveway lined with rhododendron, birch, and maple. The driveway winds to the left. We pass several white wooden buildings and a barn and look down on a little lake and beyond that what I assume to be the St. Joseph, which flows slowly, muddily past gently sloping white-fenced fields (in the Kentucky tradition). Despite the heat and drought, there's something about this place that feels downright ideal: a picture-postcard of an American farm. We pull behind the almost modest two-story white frame house and park between a shining blue Cadillac and a brown and beige convertible Rolls-Royce. Ali's Winnebago is to our left in front of a big children's playground with a slide that's probably thirty feet high, a carousel, and park-sized swings that have recently been painted candy-apple red.

A tall, strong, light-skinned woman maybe a few years younger than me and dressed in a flowing beige cotton tunic greets us at the back screen door. "Hi, I'm Lonnie Ali," she says, offering me a tentative business-style handshake before she hugs Rahaman. It's easy to understand Lonnie's reticence when shaking hands: Ali has been taken so many times by so very many hustlers. Oh, what she must have witnessed living with the world's most famous (and accessible) soft touch.

Like Ali's mom, Lonnie's oval face is splashed with a galaxy of freckles, and her loosely pinned-back hair has an aura of redness about it. She has an astute yet girlish and musical voice, slightly exophthalmic eyes and, like her husband, a dead-on, yet nonjudgmental, way of looking at you.

We enter the house through a back porch, then a small kitchen with yellow linoleum floors and countertops, a little white wooden table, and knotted oak cabinets exactly like those in the kitchen in my dad's house. "Muhammad's asleep," Lonnie says.

She's the first Ali intimate I've heard call him by

his first name. She leads us into a large, warmly lit den with white walls, thick wheat-colored carpet, a stereo, overstuffed beige couches, a silent TV that takes up almost one whole wall, a mahogany desk covered with stack upon stack of blue and yellow and green and pink pamphlets of some type, and, against the side of the steps that lead upstairs, a big ornate dark wooden trunk on which a small brass plaque under the lock reads MUHAMMAD ALI MAGIC.

Lonnie says, "This heat bothers Muhammad. Tires him out. And it's bad for his bronchitis."

Bronchitis. Maybe that explains Ali's cough. And this heat: It tires me, too. Even in here out of the sun, it's maybe ninety degrees. A small rotating fan whirs on the kitchen table and a large green model clunks and rattles in the window behind the desk. It's pretty surprising that a guy who has made probably a hundred million dollars in his career lives in a house that hasn't been air-conditioned. And although the den furnishings are comfortable, they certainly aren't posh.

Rock and I take seats on a sofa and Lonnie steps out to the kitchen, returning with sweating glasses of lemonade. We sip our drinks and talk about the *New York Times* piece, as well as a *Sports Illustrated* cover story that I had shown Ali the April day that it had first appeared on newsstands and that Lonnie and Rock and I now agree was anything but fair to him. I ask Lonnie how she reacts when people treat Ali as a cripple.

"People believe what they read in the press," she

says. Then: "I just wish some writer could tell the truth about Muhammad, could find a way to get to his soul."

As she says this, I silently resolve to write the best Ali stories that anyone will ever publish: *I will become the Greatest Ali Writer of All Times—I outflash Hunter S. Thompson with a pyrotechnic (non-drug-fried) display of lexical skill. Arms pointed skyward in victory, my feet explode into the shuffle over the fallen Norman Mailer. Twenty thousand fans in the Garden erupt into singular applause as I hop through the ropes, leaving the ring with the protection of New York's finest.* At the moment, all I need is a little cooperation from *Esquire* to help me get started on that crusade.

We finish our lemonades and chat for a while, then Lonnie says that she has laundry to do and, as she escorts us back through the kitchen, suggests that Rock and I take a tour of the farm while Muhammad sleeps. "Floyd's out there somewhere," she tells Rock, motioning toward a window and in the direction of the barn. "Maybe he can show Davy around."

I can't help but chuckle. She looks at me, wondering why I've laughed. I don't want to tell her the reason. "I'm sorry," I say. "It's just that it amazes me how kind you all are, how much you accept strangers into your lives."

Truth is, I'm not surprised by that at all. How could I be? This is the family of Muhammad Ali, who feels he belongs (*wants* to belong) to every man, woman, and child in the world. The real reason I laughed is this: *Davy!* she said. *Davy!* Lonnie called me. Not Davis. Not David, either, or even Dave or Dennis, all of which I'm used to being mistakenly tagged.

Nobody's ever called me Davy. At least no one since my great-grandmother Mandy, who, when I was little, laughed her bold, sweet, crackling laugh and called me "Davy Crockett." But Mandy's been gone for more than a decade. And I'm thirty-seven years old. *Davy!* A grown man being called Davy. I think I like it. It has sort of a family resonance about it.

Rock opens the back door and the heat slaps us flat on our faces. As we walk across the asphalt parking area, I ask if it's true that this was originally Al Capone's farm. Rock shakes his head as if I'm the only Ali fan he's ever listened to. "Man, it's hard to believe you sometimes," he says, which I take to mean that the Capone rumor is true.

We move into the scant relief of dappled shade from expansive oaks beside the barn. With a creak, Rock pushes open the long, rusted barn door and we step through a weak shaft of light in which dust motes shine. It's so bright in the sun that it's hard to see in the barn, a little like putting your head under clouded water. After a few seconds, I make out shapes; within a half minute, apparitions take form. Hanging on rough exposed beams and walls and littering the ground are framed sixties and seventies paintings and photographs of Ali and a few tarnished trophies.

"Looks better, don't it?" comes a voice from behind.

"Floyd Bass, my man," Rock says before he whips around, grinning his grin.

I turn and see a figure in dirty gray pinstripe button-up coveralls standing in direct light just outside the doorway. "If you don't know Ali," Floyd Bass says as he pulls off a brown work glove, then snaps a greasy pink rag from his pocket, "it's hard to understand why he don't care about this stuff."

Bass moves out of the sun and across the packed dirt floor and with the rag knocks a fat brown spider and its web from a grungy loving cup that bears the inscription ATHLETE OF THE CENTURY—MUHAM-MAD ALI.

Floyd Bass doesn't look much like a Floyd, I think. A guy with Floyd Bass's countenance should have a name like Isaiah or Abraham or Hezekiah. Or maybe something simpler but no less profound: Silas or Walker or Will or Jude. The name Floyd seems pretty mundane for such an intriguing-looking man.

Floyd Bass has smooth, glowing, unwrinkled skin; shining eyes the hue of sand and October sea; a curly halo of slightly receded hair that has gone prematurely white (as if it has been illuminated); a short, round beard that is the color of both shadow and light; a slight, perpetual-seeming crinkled smile; a whisper-soft, even-timbred voice; and a general demeanor that suggests he has visited the mountain and come down changed. How could anyone look and sound more like the perfect handyman for Ali the mystic?

"Until I started working with this," Bass says of the

memorabilia around us, "it was all stacked over in that corner, all covered with pigeon shit." He points to empty nests in the rafters. "Even now, when most of his stuff's long gone, when some fan shows up with a wife and kids, Ali'll give 'em a trophy or some old gloves or a painting or somethin'. He does it all the time, even now. It's amazing he's got anything left."

Rahaman introduces me and asks Floyd Bass if he has time to show us the farm. Bass takes off his other work glove and stuffs the pair in his right pocket. "I'll give you the ten-dollar tour," he says, smiling as if this is an inside joke.

He leads us through a side door and past a pen of shaved sheep panting in the heat, then through a scorched yet sweet-hay-smelling pasture and down to the narrow river, where Bass shows us that it curves around three sides of the Ali property, and tells us that the farm is eighty-eight acres of the best bottom-land he's seen anywhere.

Headed back toward the main house, we climb a gently hilled pasture through hip-high grass and a tangle of blackberry bushes. As we climb, my right tibia begins its electric, shinsplint ache. We crest the hill and I notice that my jeans and canvas shoes are flecked with hundreds of grass seeds and beggar's-lice. Despite the pain in my shin and the relentless heat, I find myself smiling and remembering a recent TV program on which Stephen Jay Gould or some-body like him claimed that there were over fifteen hundred pounds of termites for every person on the

planet. And that, like the rest of us oxygen con-
sumers, those little guys fart methane, which balances
the carbon content of the atmosphere and keeps the
world from incinerating itself. I don't know whether
or not to believe this. It sounds ridiculously hopeful.
But that doesn't matter. There's a kind of comfort in
the idea, anyway.

We step onto the driveway and pick beggar's-lice
and shake other seeds from our clothes, then I start
for the house, anxious to see if Ali's awake. "Whoa,
not so fast. We've got one more stop," Bass says,
winking as he turns toward four white shacks near
the curve in the highway.

Except for being smaller, the buildings remind me
of the ones you see in old B westerns, movies set in
frontier ghost towns with names like Tombstone. We
head for the next-to-the-last shack, which has a va-
cant horse stall attached to the right side and double
swinging doors not unlike those to a saloon. There's a
window near the center of both splintered and crumbling doors; the glass on each has been painted black.
The only other window that I can see is around the
left side of the building; it's smeared with orangish
mud and has been covered from the inside with
sheets of newsprint that make it impossible to peer
within. Bass pulls a heavy jangle of keys from a silver
chain hooked to a loop that's attached to his left
pocket, and finds a big old rusted iron key, which he
inserts in the blackened lock. He leans his right
shoulder and foot into the left side of the door, shoves

it open, and suffers a shower of rotted wood before he steps to the side, waving Rock and me through.

Chipped floorboards, water-damaged Sheetrock walls, no visible electric lighting. And no tommy guns left by a former owner. There is, however, a heavy bag, its big black leather bulk hanging sure and straight and silent in the center of the room. No! Not just *a bag*—this is The Bag, the Famous Ali Heavy Bag, the one he had custom-made for the Foreman bout (bags packed in the usual way damaged his delicate hands when he punched) and that he continued to use through the Thrilla in Manila and for the rest of his fistic career.

Near the rear of the stubby room, opposite the big bag, is a black wooden platform, from which hangs a brand-spanking-new shining fire-engine-red Everlast 4204 Astro, one of the fastest full-sized speed bags in existence, its bladder freshly pumped with air and ready to sing. Across the floor from the bags is what's left of a twenty-foot ring, the canvas near-filthy with ancient sweat and farm dirt, the formerly flexible blue plastic covers on the rough braided ropes now brittle, ripped and fading, the ropes themselves sagging into one another like kudzu vines after the first winter frost. Could this be the same ring in which, several lives ago, I had sparred with Ali when he ached with beauty, and from which I was led looking freshly electrocuted?

"Mosta this stuff came from Deer Lake when the camp people took over," Bass explains, still brushing wood particles from his coveralls.

"What camp people?" I ask.

"The old boxing gear got moved out and the training camp's turned into a center for abused kids," he says. "I'm not sure anybody anywhere likes children as much as Ali."

I nod. "His radar sure is tuned to kids," I say. "Does Ali really use this stuff?"

"Sometimes," says Bass.

"This past spring," I say, "I saw him box a couple rounds with this pretty good amateur, and he politely trashed the kid. I had no idea that was still in him. You remember that, Rock?"

"He'll never give it up," Rahaman says. "Not all the way he won't."

"Let me tell you about Ali," Bass offers, sounding playful yet serious in a professorial tone: His is the voice of the keeper of tender mysteries. "About a year ago—last July, I believe it was—there was a tribute for Ali down at the Community Center. Place was packed. Looked like everybody in Michigan showed up. Ali signed autographs for every person who came, and hugged and kissed everybody in the room. Ten, maybe twelve kids from my boxing team turned out. When Ali got ready to leave, he loaded all the kids up in the Winnebago and brought 'em all back home. When we pulled in the driveway, it was just about this time of day—the streetlight beside the garage had just come on. Ali went to the barn and he came back wearin' this pair of beat-up brown gloves from one of his fights or someplace. He got those kids out in the driveway and gave every one of 'em a coupla rounds with him. After a while, I got sleepy and went to my pickup. I wanted to leave, tried to leave—even started the engine—but, but . . . I—I just couldn't. I sat there watching and just couldn't go nowhere. Sat leanin' over the steering wheel, starin' at Ali and all my kids while they moved around that lighted, sparklin' asphalt until past midnight."

Bass's story motivates me. Wanting to feel an even greater connection with Ali, I step to the Champ's renowned heavy bag and spring punches into its musty old hide as Bass and Rock watch. With each technique thrown, I imagine that prisms of light follow my fists. "Not bad," Bass says, "for a white boy."

Rock thinks this Ali-inspired line is funny as can be. He laughs and laughs and makes a hissing sound between his teeth.

We lock the gym and Bass asks if I'd mind driving down the road to St. Joseph to grab a soda or something. "Don't worry about missing him," he says of Ali. "He won't wake up no time soon."

Although Bass's comment makes me a little uncomfortable and I remain uneasy about leaving, we clamber into the Volvo and drive up the long driveway and out onto a scarred and pitted country highway, past the campus of Andrews University (to which, Bass says, Ali often walks to talk with/debate/evangelize seminary students), then grove after grove of dwarf apple and peach trees, grape orchards, and the smell of fields being fertilized with manure. We pass the St. Joseph River yet again, round a curve, and suddenly we're smack in the middle of a long, low, garish retail strip.

Bass suggests we stop at the St. Joseph McDonald's. Inside, we order fries and sodas, a fish sandwich for Rahaman, chicken for Bass. We take seats at a purple and yellow plastic table and I ask Bass how he met Ali. "I was livin' in the Silicon Valley," he says. "Made me a fortune in microchips—and lost it. Got real depressed. Decided to come back home, thought that might improve my luck. But it didn't."

As he's speaking, Bass's face becomes incongruous with what he's saying: His smile goes crinkled, fuzzy, and enigmatic; his skin takes on a sheen and becomes more richly colored; and although he doesn't move in his seat, his features edge themselves almost imperceptibly toward his listeners. "Moved in with my mother," he tells us. "Can you imagine that? A man my age. Didn't want a job, couldn't find one anyway, just about decided I'd go over to the oven, turn on the gas, and stick my head in it. That's when I read in the paper that Ali was movin' to Berrien Springs full-time. For years, everybody knew he had the farm— he'd come sometimes to rest up. A few days after that story, I ran into him here, right here under the Golden Arches."

Bass must see my surprise at the revelation that he met the Greatest of All Times while eating at a McDonald's. "Ali knows there's always people here," he explains, "always somebody to talk to. He walks over and gets a hot chocolate or a coffee, maybe a sundae."

"Walks!" I say, my reaction just about incredulous.

"You mean from the farm?" I had looked at the odometer as we wheeled into the parking lot: It's over eleven miles from the Ali place to here. And that's taking the main road. Getting off the highway, I'm pretty sure the distance would be farther.

"Yep," says Bass. "Coupla, maybe three times a week when he's home." At great-granddaddy Ali's pace, these McDonald's trips must take most of the daylight hours—especially since he is, after all, who he is: His progress certainly gets blunted every couple hundred yards (mostly to his delight, I'd bet) by people who stop their vehicles to say hello or ask for autographs.

"In this weather," I say, "does he do it? Does he still walk all this distance?"

Bass nods. "None of us want him to, least of all Lonnie. If the sun don't get him, we all worry he'll get run over. But Ali's just gonna do what Ali's gonna do. I tried to tag along a few times, thought he might want the company. After a mile or two, he sent me home. Said he wanted to be alone.

"Anyway," Bass goes on, "I met him here and we talked and I told him I used to box. Told him I became a civil rights activist because of him. Asked if he thought he might need some help around the place. I came over that Saturday and raked a few leaves and burned the piles. Then I started doing a few odds and ends for him, not takin' money for my work. Next thing I know, I'm workin' thirty hours a week."

Bass laughs, scoots his chair back, gets up. Standing over me, his face goes even brighter than it had already been. "I swear to you," he says, "that man saved my life." He turns from the table and, as he does so, I note that he is bald in precisely the spot Franciscan brothers shave their crowns to provide an unobstructed pathway through which to receive heavenly illumination.

He quickly returns with salt and pepper shakers in his right fist. "Every day," he says, "that man makes me glad to be alive, glad I know him."

This sounds like something Floyd Bass has wanted to say for a while. I find myself nodding in agreement. "Hell, I'm glad to be part of the same species as him," Bass says. "I tell you, that man's a real live angel."

"Yeah, yeah," Rahaman says with tartar sauce in his mustache. Chomping on a bite of fish sandwich, he, too, is nodding. "He's my own brother." He swallows hard. "I mean, I know he got the same daddy as me, and the same mama—and he come from between her legs. My whole life I been watchin' him—watched him get exactly where he is right now. But that's the way I feel about him, too."

What a life Ali has had. I recall a TV documentary in honor of Copland on his eighty-fifth birthday. "There is no greater reward than having been able to make my living creating something that will outlive me," the old composer told an interviewer. Our species has perhaps an innate desire for continuance. Most of us grope for immortality in religion, through our children, in the possessions we collect, in the names we give fellowships and buildings, through our work, on tombstones. Artists grabble for immortality through art and/or fame. The first place Muhammad Ali groped for his was through the renown he garnered in the ring. In the history of the world, Ali is more famous than anyone else has been in his or her own lifetime. Way back in 1975, Wilfrid Sheed wrote, with more than a little awe in his prose, that Ali's likeness hung in African mud huts. And surely this was (and is) true. Just as certainly, it hung on walls in Kiev, Detroit, London, Mobile, Kuala Lumpur, and L.A., as well as in Tokyo, Cleveland, Beijing, and Mexico City. Ali became known and honored in nearly every nation, city, town, and village on the planet.

When I was a student at East Carolina, a visiting poet told a story of a trip to the Sahara. He and his wife hadn't seen anyone for miles and miles, days and days, dune after dune. They passed a herd of goats and a boy of about ten years. In Arabic the boy asked the poet where he lived. When the poet answered, the boy enthusiastically repeated "America," and danced in a circle around his small herd. "Muhammad Ali! Muhammad Ali!" he shouted.

The poetry of the name. Muhammad Ali. It doesn't much matter that the words are Islamic. The music of the name itself, the sheer beauty of the sound, is what's most interesting. As long as there are human beings, it's likely that the name will be spoken.

Inevitability. "The whole point of composing," Copland told fellow composer David Diamond, "is to feel inevitable." It now often feels as if Muhammad Ali had to come along when he did.

What would Ali himself have to say about this? Ever since I began watching him, he has always carried himself as if he is centered in his own destiny, as if he is doing that which he is intended to do. Ali has been a creature of earth and of sky: He has acted as though he owns everything, and nothing. He has claimed to be the Most Important Person to have lived, and the simplest of men. He has seemed the world's wisest man, and some kind of virgin.

These things considered, Ali's sojourns to the Golden Arches, to that global emissary of sales hyperbole ("Billions and Billions Served Worldwide"), make perfect sense. And even the Greatest Kickboxing Writer of All Times could scarcely invent a more appropriate location for Ali's monk-handyman, Floyd Bass, to propose the divinity of Planet Earth's First Truly International Human.

Fourteen

As we leave McDonald's, Bass asks to swing by the house of the county sheriff, a short, round, red-cheeked man of maybe fifty-five, who leans across a banister on his front porch and promises he'll have deputies look out for Ali. "We'll convince him there're better places to take his exercise than a patch of skinny country highway," he tells Bass.

I understand and admire Bass's and the sheriff's concern for Ali. Like so many folks, however, they're treating Ali as if he isn't capable of making his own decisions, as if his malady has robbed him of some vital and essential part of himself. The effect of their kindly yet covert act, as has so often been true throughout Ali's life, is to deprive him of the opportunity simply to *be*. Not an hour before, Bass had theorized Ali's celestiality; now he has suggested that the man—oops! angel—can't make it across the road on his own. This isn't any reason for me to get pissed. These guys hope to keep Ali from being squashed by a careening eighteen-wheeler, from becoming the Most Famous Roadkill of All Times. Yet, to me their reaction seems unfortunate.

Until I stop to consider the situation from another perspective: Bass and the sheriff, although they may not be able to say it, or feel no need to do so, simply wish to protect that which they regard as, well, if not sacrosanct, at least precious. They want to do what they believe is best for someone they (we all!) care about. And for sure I don't have any quarrel with that. There are so many ways to think about most everything. And none of them is nearly as round as the reality. After a while, it seems marvelously futile to say you know much of anything about anything.

When we return to the house, Bass gets in his rusty old pickup and heads for home. I pull two choice items from the Volvo's backseat for Ali to autograph and promise myself that I won't take advantage of his munificence by asking him to sign anything again for a long, long time. As Rock and I go in the back, even though it's been a good while since sunset, there's a note from Lonnie on the door that says she's at the grocery store. Inside, Rock picks up a remote control from the coffee table; the TV blinks on to CNN. I'm not interested in watching: My antennae are on Ali alert.

Within minutes, a pair of big flat bran-colored feet

slowly descend the staircase, followed by the torso and head of the world's best-known man, who's wearing wrinkled black slacks and a freshly starched black safari shirt that has a yellow laundry tag stapled to a lower buttonhole. His face is swollen and his hair needs combing. He sucks a deep breath. "My man," he says, seeming to summon language from an almost forgotten recess.

He gives me his hand and, as we shake, tickles the inside of my palm with his middle finger. I laugh and say, "Man, you never quit, do you?"

Without acknowledging Rahaman or saying anything further to me, Ali wades away to the kitchen, returning with a sloshing white mug of very black coffee, which he carefully places on the table before he falls back on the sofa between his brother and me. He doesn't look at either of us, but leans forward, reaching for a sugar bowl on the table. He tries to clear his throat, turns his eyes toward me, and points questioningly at his cup.

"No, thanks, Champ," I tell him. "Rock and I drank about a gallon of iced tea maybe an hour ago."

Ali nods, snorts, coughs his wet cough, takes a spoon from the sugar bowl, and dumps spoon- after spoonful into his cup and onto the table, probably seven or eight mountainous servings altogether. After a fat noisy slurp, he sits his dripping mug back on the table.

"Glad you're here, glad to see you," he says, and gives my leg the gentlest squeeze in the hollow right above the knee. He gets up again and walks over to his desk, motioning for me to follow.

"Sign a thousanda these a day. Take some, give 'em to your friends." He picks up a thick stack of little green pamphlets and hands them to me. I look down at the pieces of paper in my hand. IS JESUS REALLY GOD? reads the thick bold script in the center of the page. Above Jesus' name is Ali's signature and the month and year, with a space left in the middle for the date. "If anybody else tried to give these to people, they wouldn't take 'em or they'd throw 'em away," he says. "I sign 'em and they take 'em home and keep 'em."

He grabs a big gold permanent marker, from which he removes the cap, then takes his seat behind the desk, waiting for me. I'm a little startled by this reaction—that he knows I want him to autograph some stuff—but I unfold a two-by-three-foot poster that used to hang on my bedroom wall in Daddy's house and I spread the poster across Ali's desk. It's a copy of the famous photograph in which Ali contorts George Foreman's features with a staff-straight right (a halo of sweat lifts from Foreman's face with the impact of the blow; Ali glows like an enlightened being in the paintings in the *Bhagavad-gita*). Ali stares at the photo an interminable moment; it's not hard to tell that he doesn't want to sign. Some part of him is no longer proud of the ways in which he has hurt other human beings.

"Davis Miller is my name," I say. "D-A-V-I-S." As he continues to hesitate, I open my mouth to tell him that I understand, that he doesn't have to sign. But now his hand is on the paper. "To Davis Miller," he writes, "LOVE, Muhammad Ali, 8-3-89."

He carefully refolds the poster and hands it to me, then autographs the fight program I've been keeping since Lyn and I tried to get married at the Shavers bout. He snaps the top back on his marker and pushes it to the only corner of the desk not inhabited by Muslim tracts.

"You believe in ghosts?" he asks, for no reason that I can determine. I could tell him a scary story or two, but decide I won't.

"No," I say.

"I'll show you a ghost, I'll make you believe." From his magic trunk he pulls a thin white cloth, which he places over the spilled coffee and sugar. He waves his hands across the table and says, "Arise, ghost, arise," in a foggy-sounding voice. The cloth quavers and a coffee-stained peak shakingly appears in the middle.

"Told you there's a ghost in the room," he says.

I ask: "Do *you* believe in ghosts?"

"Do you?" Ali says.

"Yes," I say. I study his face. He doesn't seem surprised. "You're a ghost," I say, "or I guess I mean the images people have of you—what they, and me, and even you, say you represent—those are ghosts. And I'm a ghost, too. The way I want—no, *feel a need* to get something about you on paper, to write the best story in me, and have it carry on for years after my body is gone. That's being a ghost. But it's not the only way I'm one. We're all ghosts. Walking, talking spirits. All of us. In countless ways. All the time."

"*Maannn*, that's powerful," he says. "Heavy. You oughta write a book."

Fifteen

No relief yet from the drought. Lyn gives me the necessary quiet to rewrite "My Dinner with Ali"— and takes respite from the heat—by going with the children to the neighborhood pool all day, every day. The lifeguard, a fun and hopeful kid named Brian, who studies American lit at Western Kentucky University and who at night sometimes comes by for beers and writing chat, teaches Johanna to swim and does an expert job of keeping daring-do Isaac from the bottom of eight feet of water. Lyn and the kids have a fine, relaxing time, returning home most evenings with broad bright smiles and eventually with nut-brown skin and sun-ripe hair. And they spend *nada dinero*, which is almost exactly what we have left in the bank. Yet I feel guilty that they're out every day soaking up rays. After all, the ozone-depleted Sol-shine ain't exactly healthy for anyone's skin. I ask Lyn to buy a bottle of sunscreen, but she says we can't afford the five dollars. You know, if all things have Buddha-nature, if "God" is omnipresent, some of this interconnectedness stuff sort of sucks big-time. Or at least the essence of things seems weird: Sun feels wonderful on skin as it cooks the moisture from cutaneous cells and propagates melanomas; vanilla ice cream slides soothingly down throats on the way to causing acid rebound and clogging arteries. Boxing skills promote coordinative elegance, a heightened awareness of the senses, and occasionally even pull someone from the swamp of his life—only to take all this away somewhere down the line. Feels almost insidious, doesn't it?

Anyway, while Lyn and the kids are getting smilingly fried at the pool, I'm plunking away at my mom's old typewriter. Every couple hours, I break for a round or two on the bag or maybe a few abdominal exercises. My weight's down about ten pounds since I left video, and you can see little cuts in my abs for the first time in years. I take time out to make videocassette copies of all the Ali fights I have and mail them to Ali and Lonnie, Mrs. Clay and Rock. Lonnie sends a thank-you note. "Usually, when Muhammad gets anything like this," she writes, "he gives them away. I'll be sure to keep these safe."

When I'm pleased with "My Dinner with Ali," when I'm certain that rewriting didn't take anything from the flow, I get the story off in the mail once again.

Still no luck with jobs. It seems that every promising position I circle in the classifieds and make an appointment to apply for, when I arrive someplace to be interviewed, ends up being a disguised Amway distributorship or door-to-door water-filter sales.

Daddy has called several times and asked us to move home. My grandmother died this past spring and he offered to let us stay rent-free in her house until we sell our place. I'm so fidgety as I wait to hear back from *Esquire* and everything's so ugly here with the drought—brown and shriveled and cracked and just horrible—that I'm more than ready to escape. Lyn and I decide that I'll take Johanna with me to Winston-Salem so our daughter can start school at the beginning of the semester and that Lyn and Isaac will stay in Kentucky to get the house ready to go on the market.

I leave the number at my grandmom's on my editor's voice mail and spend the weekend stuffing the Volvo with Johanna's books and toys, her clothes and mine, the little stereo from the study, and the telephone answering machine, making sure I won't miss the call that tells the date that "My Dinner" will be published. I don't know if I'll ever see Ali again. Not living in Louisville, it seems unlikely. Still, what I've had feels like enough. After all, how many of us ever get to spend the time with their childhood idol that I have with mine?

By Monday morning, the only place left to cram

anything else in the car is on the floorboard on Johanna's side, where I reverentially place the most recent copy of "My Dinner," the autographed Ali memorabilia, and the typewriter. Lyn brings out a grocery bag of sandwiches, fruit, cookies, crackers, and a big thermos of lemonade for the drive home, which I also place on the floorboard. We pay one last visit to the Great Wide Muddy, where we snap photos of boats on the water and the kids picking up clamshells. Then we're off.

I'm glad to get some time alone with Johanna. With Lyn having left me six weeks after Johanna was born and then with me working so many hours and toiling to learn to write with any and every moment I could wrangle since we've been back together (and my frustrations not making me the most fun person in North America on those rare days that I take off), my daughter and I've never been very close.

Johanna and I hold hands, count cows, listen to music, stop beside the road for naps, and talk about seeing her old friends when we get to Winston-Salem. Coming across the mountains, right after we pass through Asheville, the thermos tips over on the floorboard and spills sticky, acidic lemonade all over Ali's face and right fist in the poster he signed when I was in Berrien Springs. Johanna rescues Ali's image from the lemonade puddle and I quickly pull to the shoulder and dry the poster with a bath towel. I'll do a more thorough job when we get to Winston, but even if I manage to clean the poster well enough to "preserve" it, the acid will eventually eat away his signature as well as his image. But then, if the lemonade had not been spilled, the poster surely wouldn't've survived more than a few human lifetimes, anyway. So much for the theory that immortality may be attained through art.

Is it futile to strive for immortality? Certainly. Is it in some way "wrong," or "wrong"-minded? Given that our throb for continuance is in and of the nature of being human, that it's something we're born with, maybe that's an irrelevant question. "That from which one can deviate is not the Tao," wrote Lao Tzu. Yet, the perils of being ambitious, of having ambitions—one of the most common manifestations of our innate yearning for immortality—are well understood. There's a kind of myopia associated with being ambitious, an emphasis not on the world and on beings around us, but on the Self, as well as a tendency to be less than kind. Hence, another of the lessons of Ali's life: Look what happens when you regularly punch folks in the head and say you're better than them—smarter, prettier, faster, more graceful—that you're the Greatest Who Has Ever Been. Consider the karma that finds you when you diminish the humanness of other men, when you attempt to disconnect yourself from others and tout your own superiority (while making millions of dollars) by calling them names such as the Acorn (Earnie Shavers), the Big, Ugly Bear (Sonny Liston), the Mummy (George Foreman), the Washerwoman (George Chuvalo), the Walrus (Leon Spinks), the

(Scared) Rabbit (Floyd Patterson), the Peanut (Larry Holmes), and of course, the Gorilla (Joe Frazier). Muhammad Ali, this otherwise wondrously tender man, turned folks into "its" to inflict harm upon them.

At dusk, headed east on I-40, Johanna and I drive from dry road onto a stretch where it has just rained. The pavement is wet, the sun is already out again, shadows from trees and cars are sharp, precise; I watch the sunset reflected in water on the road and beaming in a million wet blades of fescue. I think about the aura around Ali, the way his skin seems always to shine, even now, even through his malady. And I consider the possibility that what we see is not the person glowing, but the individual connecting with a greater glow.

A few fat drops of rain hit the Volvo's windshield. It's the first precipitation we've seen all summer. "Yay, Johanna, it's raining," I say, and turn to look at her. She hasn't lifted her head from her Judy Blume book. Well, I guess you can't expect a seven-year-old to share your excitement for something like a little water in the air. I get off of the interstate at the next exit, slow to twenty, roll down my window, and stick my head way, way out, letting rain strike my face.

"Daddy, *Daddy*," Johanna squeals almost hysterically, sounding disturbingly like her mother when she's upset at me. "Daddy, what are you *doing*?"

I tell her I'm enjoying the rain.

"Daddy, will you *please* get back in the car?" she

pleads. "Daddy, this is *dangerous!* Daddy, *Daddy!* . . . Daddy, you are *so weird.*"

The closer we've gotten to Winston-Salem, the better I've felt. The road ahead is empty. It's significantly greener in western North Carolina than in Louisville or in Michigan. Pastures, trees, and roadside grass are soft-looking and are the hue of sherbet. With my head out the window, I smell rain and grass and hemlock and listen to the *shoosh*ing of tires on the wet pavement. Isn't it odd that the best things, the ones that feel most real, are often those that also seem most dreamlike? What a nirvana-moment. I don't know if anything could be much better than this. If there is nirvana, I'm convinced that this is where it is: in the moment. Reveling in the senses without talking—how glorious. Language sometimes feels like wearing a pair of stiff leather shoes a couple sizes too small.

Who knows how much (if any) of this stuff I've been thinking and writing about Ali is true? TRUTH: Nah; truth: well, maybe. Perhaps the ever-changing "truth" about Ali is a matter of perspective. "The frog in the well cannot know the immensity of the sky." That which was considered to be the most solid Ali reporting thirty, twenty, even ten years ago crumbles like sandstone when read today.

As the rain starts to hurt my face, I pull my head in and look at Johanna. She's rolled down her window and her head is raised to the sky. Her eyes are closed, parts of her face are red with pelting rain, parts are brown with sun she's had this summer, her ears are a little purple, as are her lips. She looks almost exactly like photos of my mother as a young girl. Johanna's face is soaked, her curls have softened, and they cascade down the back of her T-shirt. She seems to be enjoying herself as much as I had.

Sixteen

We've decided to kill the story," the editor says in a manner that might most kindly be called officious. "I'll be sure you get your kill fee quick. Sorry this took so long."

"Kill fee?" I say. "What do you mean, 'kill fee'?"

"Read your contract," he says. "We don't run the piece, you don't get full payment. We owe you, uh . . . let's see. What were we paying you? . . . Yeah, twenty-five hundred. Twenty-five hundred times fifteen percent. We owe you . . . four hundred seventy-five dollars. Oops, excuse me. Three-seventy-five. I'll see to it that accounting gets your check out tomorrow."

I hang up the phone wondering how anybody named after my all-time favorite candy bar could act like such a jerk. I guess it happens for the reason any of us become most anything we become: fear. We're all so scared. It's difficult to overstate what fear makes us do. Makes us act, makes us not act, say no, say yes, make no decision at all, join the Republican party, get married, write stories, jump around in a prize ring, start wars, heal the sick. Makes us (sort of) believe we know something special, makes us think we're better than others, and makes us feel that we're worthless and can't do anything at all. Makes us do just about every ole thing people do.

"I knew this would happen," says my wife, the world-class optimist, when I call to tell the news. "But it was worth a try, I guess. Have you had any luck finding a job?"

Not yet, I tell her. "Something's going to work out with this anyway, Lyn," I say, meaning the story, my writing. "I'm sure of it."

"I've called the hospital," she says. "They'll give me my job back. At my old rate of pay—five-forty-three per hour."

Before I took the district manager's position, Lyn filed papers in medical records at the hospital. It was a crummy job she never much liked and I figured there was no way she'd have to do it again. I'm grateful, though, that she's willing to go back to such a dead-end position.

I ask about unemployment checks. She says the first one has come and she has money for gas and groceries.

"I'll talk with Video Village," I say. "I don't think

they need a manager here, but maybe there'll be something for me. I'll let you know."

"You don't have to call me back. We won't have to spend money on the call," says my wife. "Isaac and I are coming home next weekend. I've told the hospital that I can start work the following Monday."

I'm glad that Lyn and Isaac are on the way, but this money situation is getting, if not dire, then borderline desperate. I don't want to lose the house or the car and I'm not going to take any more money from Daddy. Besides, I'm not sure he has it to give, anyway. If he did, he would've retired by now. It's been years since he's found pleasure in his job. In the weeks since Johanna and I have been home, we've been taking some of our meals with him, meeting at restaurants when he gets off work. He looks so dragged out and just through with it after a day at the plant. As soon as I make it as a writer, I'll retire him. Buy him a little place in the mountains or at the beach where he can take it easy and fish and sit in the sun and enjoy himself.

I'm not about to tell Daddy that "My Dinner with Ali" has been rejected. I'll wait until I sell the story somewhere before I let him know. Lyn and I need the money so bad I don't have time to futz around with another New York magazine. I call the *Courier-Journal* and ask for the Sunday magazine editor's name and address. Within the hour, before I have time to think about it and change my mind, I mail "My Dinner with Ali" back up to Louisville with a copy of the cover letter I'd written for the *Esquire* editor and a handwritten note saying that *Esquire* has decided to kill the piece.

I receive a call in less than a week. "This is an amazing story," says the editor. "We want to use it as our cover piece next week."

Next week. Wow. "How much can you pay?" I ask.

"We've come up with some special money for you. More than we've ever paid. Four hundred dollars."

I don't say anything. I guess he senses my disappointment.

"We know it's not magazine money," he says, "but for a newspaper, it's very good."

If this is considered good, how can I possibly make a living writing? This was two months solid work. But, even though it ain't Daddy's retirement money, it'll pay the bills for a week. Just as important, the story will see print. I'll be able to show it to family and friends and it'll run in Louisville, where Ali's mom and Rock, his family and friends, my former store managers, and Ali himself will surely see it. I tell myself that this is the most important thing, after all.

Lyn calls again on Wednesday, saying that her parents have invited her and the kids to their beach cottage for Labor Day, this weekend. The Harrises will pay for the trip, she says. She'll follow them to Winston on Sunday and will start work on Monday.

The Harrises will pick up Johanna from school to-

morrow on the way to the coast. This is very welcome
news. I've got an idea for another story that I'm anxious to start on: a piece of fiction about a teenage girl
who works in a video store and dreams of becoming a
world-champion kickboxer. I decide to celebrate Lyn
coming home and selling "My Dinner" by buying a
copy of the new Pat Metheny CD, *Letter from Home*,
and a whole ream of paper. I'm so excited to get a
long weekend alone to listen to music, to work out,
and to begin a new story that I almost forget to play
messages on the answering machine.

Seventeen

The voice is so low and broken I'm not sure I'd recognize the caller if he didn't say who he was.

"Son, this is your dad," the voice says slowly, falling off near the end of the sentence. "Give me a call when you get in."

I rewind and play the message again. I've never heard Daddy sound anything like this. No positive quality at all in his voice. Nothing playful.

Instead of calling back, I drive to his house, parking in the grass to the right of the driveway, between the dogwood tree and the snowball bush he and my mother planted the spring we moved in. Opening the back door, I look into the den. He's in his easy chair across from the TV, a John Wayne western shooting up the room, his hand latched around a can of Diet Coke. He must drink twenty of these miserable things a day. He's dressed like he's ready to go to work, wearing a pair of chocolate dress slacks and a checked short-sleeve shirt.

"It's beautiful outside," I say. "Feels like fall."

"Every time I've gone to the hospital," says my father, "it's been weather like this. So clear it hurts your eyes. Clear as the mornin' the space shuttle blew up."

I eye Daddy hard. Except in the ring, I've never seen anyone look the way he does right now. Shocked to the marrow. In downright awe. Yet fallen into his body. And almost entirely resigned.

"Son, my chest hurts," he says. Daddy never talks about how he feels. When you ask about his health, he always says "I'm all right," and looks away.

Now he tells me, "It hurts so bad I ain't slept since Tuesday. Don't want to go to the hospital. Don't want to die in no hospital."

His matter-of-factness stuns me so much I don't know what to say or do. So I laugh. "You're not dying," I say. "You're fine."

He stands and moves slowly to his desk. "When you need them, you'll find my papers in the bottom right drawer."

He takes a seat and writes checks for water and electric bills, for his Sears charge and MasterCard. Like he did when I was a kid, he asks me to lick stamps and seal envelopes. He hands me a check for a thousand dollars, saying that it should take care of a few things. He gets up from his chair, leaving the bills where I've placed them on the desktop.

"Dave, promise me you'll see to it that everything

goes like it should," he says, pointing at the middle of my chest, his voice slightly tremulous. "Promise you'll take care of everything."

"Of course I will," I say, laughing again. "You know that. But there's not going to be anything to take care of. You're going to be fine."

He turns his back and leaves the room. "Ambulances cost too much," he says, disappearing around the corner into the kitchen. "You take me in."

The refrigerator door closes. He comes back into sight carrying another Diet Coke. He pops the top while climbing in on the passenger's side of his Taurus wagon. The Taurus is a company vehicle. Daddy doesn't own a car.

"It's strange," he says. "Soon as I decide to go to the hospital, my chest quits hurtin'. Hadn't hurt since you came over."

Although it's almost chilly outside, Daddy flips the air conditioner on full blast. Every time I've ridden with him lately, his car has been just about frigid. I study him again, even harder: He's only fifty-nine. And except for most of his hair having gone white, he looks mid-forties, tops. He's young. And his skin's brown as teak. I'm sure he's going to be okay.

"Maybe you'll need a bypass, like Lyn's dad got. You're going to be fine."

All the way to the hospital, he doesn't say a word. As we pull into the tunnel that takes us down to the main entrance to the university medical center, he reaches for his wallet and tugs out a five-dollar bill.

"Go on and park and meet me inside," he says, pushing the bill into my palm.

Geez, he won't even let me pay for parking. He gets out and starts toward the building. I put the Taurus in drive and as I begin to pull away, decide to stop the car. I put the transmission back in park and, through the rearview mirror, take the time to watch the back of my father's head, his rounded shoulders through his checked shirt, and the soles of his leather shoes as he walks slowly toward the revolving glass door.

As Daddy signs admission papers, he seems normal as can be. Except for the tiny white pill that he pulls from his pocket and places in his mouth. An orderly brings a wheelchair to take Daddy upstairs. Daddy gives me his wallet and his health insurance card. "Call right now," he tells me, "and get approval from the insurance company. Don't want nobody to pay no bills."

I meet him in the Cardiac Care Unit. A work counter, behind which nurses, orderlies, students, and residents move, runs the length of the right side of the sixty-foot-long room. The left is divided into plastic-curtained spaces about the size of walk-in closets. At the door, a blue-uniformed nurse tells me that Daddy's space is in the right rear corner. I tell her thanks and smile what Lyn calls my "hopeless optimist smile."

A sense of the inescapable is in and of the air in CCU. Machines click and whir, pop and peep, wheeze and shudder. Walking through the room, I note that the curtains to the individual cubicles are all open. In the second booth, an old, old man, awash in flickering blue television light, is propped up in bed, his vivid fleshless face visible above the white, white sheets, his muscleless right arm limp and immobile atop the covers, the skin so thin it's translucent, purple arteries prominent even at a glance from these thirty feet away.

Daddy is stretched out in bed in a blue-striped hospital gown and his bed is cranked up high. He's hooked to a heart monitor and a couple other machines I don't recognize. His pulse is 118. That seems awfully high.

The only window is in the far left corner of the cubicle, behind his right shoulder, at just the right angle where an owl could maybe twist its neck far enough to look out. An almost pretty, red-haired nurse, or possibly she's a resident, is asking questions and writing down answers. "Are you a smoker?" she says.

"Not anymore," answers my father.

"When did you stop?" she asks.

"This morning," he says, and sort of laughs.

His questioner doesn't even smile. She makes a note, then looks at his yellowed eyes and makes another note.

She pulls up the bottom of the sheet and looks at Daddy's feet. "How long they been swollen like this?" she says, feeling his feet, ankles, and legs in a not-soothing manner.

"I don't know. A while, I guess."

I open my eyes a bit wide. This sounds significant. I stare at his feet. They're as swollen as latex gloves filled with hot water; the skin is tight and shining, painful-looking. I wish I'd noticed. I wish I'd known to notice.

"Mister . . . uh . . . Miller," she says, looking for his name on her clipboard, "tell me about the pain you're having."

"It's not pain," says Daddy, sounding almost hopeful, like maybe everything's going to be okay, after all. "Not like when I had my heart attack and it felt like somebody sittin' on my chest. And nothin' nearly bad as my kidney stones. Just tightness. That's all."

Her pen moves across the paper. "Any other problems?"

Daddy shakes his head.

"Chronic back pain. He's been having chronic back pain," I say, and smile, wanting to be helpful. She looks at me and makes a note, but doesn't return my smile. Then to my father she says: "Are you an organ donor?"

When Daddy shakes his head, she asks, "Do you want to donate your organs? At your age, your eyes probably aren't good anymore, but there may be other parts someone can use."

At your age. It goes without saying that this woman's got maybe the worst bedside manner of all times. She's treating this fine man, Roy L. Miller, as if he's part of the machinery in this room, as if he's some piece of equipment that's been programmed to talk, and which she's required to listen to, although she doesn't want to. I look at Daddy; he seems downright shocked. I'm stunned, too. Mostly not by this woman's gall—after all, there's nothing wrong with asking someone to donate his organs—but by the notion that my father could really be too old to give away his parts.

A big, balding, black orderly with a wheelchair tells Daddy he's to be taken to the third floor for chest X rays. I ask permission to push him. In the elevator and as we wait his turn in the lab, Daddy doesn't talk at all. The troubling thing, more than his silence, is his black, empty eyes: You stare into them and feel yourself falling and falling, falling away.

"When you get out of the hospital this time," I offer, hoping to cheer him, "why don't you start walking with me? We can do it together. It's time for us to start doing stuff together. I'll exercise with you. Writing's giving me the time I've never had."

Daddy doesn't say a word. Nor does he speak for the fifteen minutes or so we're in the lab. For hours after we make it back to the room, he remains silent while being poked and prodded by a procession of nurses, medical students, and residents. You don't see the emptiness in his eyes when there's anyone else around, though. He covers it up, or maybe it hides. I pull a soft-skinned, kind-acting doc to the side and tell him that Daddy believes he's dying. "There's nothing to support that in the numbers," he says. "His vital signs look great, his pulse is strong."

I tell him that I think Daddy may be depressed and that I know a little something about how that can affect you. He tells me thanks. "It's helpful to know how patients feel," he says, pushing his glasses back up on his nose. "We'll talk with him more about what we know. Build his confidence."

Throughout the afternoon, as people come and go, Daddy and I watch the weather station; a tropical storm is brewing off the South American coast. By midevening, Hugo has reached hurricane magnitude. "Look at this spiral pattern," a grinning announcer exclaims, almost caressing the satellite picture of the whirling clouds with his open right hand. "Notice how organized the eye is. Hugo looks as if it could become a very powerful storm."

I look at Daddy's watch. It's 9:25. Every few minutes I'm yawning full-bodied yawns, and my stomach has been rumbling since before dark. Daddy tells me he's okay, why don't I go home and get dinner and some sleep.

"When you come back tomorrow," he says, "how about bringing a pair of pajamas and my slippers, will you?"

I get up and go to the door.

"Do me another favor, will you, Dave?" he asks. "Don't tell your sister I'm in the hospital. I don't want to worry her."

As I'm wolfing down a sandwich, Lyn calls from a pay phone at the beach. "Just wanted to let you know we got here fine."

"Listen, I don't want to alarm you or anything," I
say, "but Daddy's in the hospital. It's his heart. I think
he's probably all right, and so does everybody at the
hospital, but he says he's dying. You might want to
think about coming to Winston early."

The other end is silent for a moment, then: "I'm
sure he's okay," Lyn says.

Surely she's right. Daddy looks and acts much
younger than Lyn's father, who's fifty-four. She and
I've figured Daddy'll outlive Mr. Harris by a decade
or two. And, like I've said, Lyn has real solid instincts for future tragedy. The doctors, the nurses,
Lyn, and me—no one feels that Daddy's in any real
trouble: I'll have another twenty years with him, for
sure. After all, that's only fair. We've both minded
our p's and q's, we live the ways we're supposed to.
That bit of heart trouble he had in the seventies,
what would anybody expect, raising a little shit like
me? But I've got it together pretty good now. I'm becoming a fully actualized man. At last I'll have the
time I've wanted to spend with Daddy. That's the
way the universe works. Live the right ways and
you're rewarded.

"Don't worry," continues my wife. "This is probably
good news. Maybe he'll finally start taking care of
himself."

"Yeah, we talked about him working out with me.
Maybe it is good news."

"I'm sure he'll be fine."

"With the holiday, there're no cardiologists around.
On Monday they'll give him a cath. See if he needs a

bypass. But I still think you might want to come on home tomorrow."

"You weren't upset when my father was in the hospital," she says, defensively. "You didn't go out of your way to see him."

She's right: I didn't. The Harrises and I've never much cared for each other. When Lyn and I started dating, they told her I was too old for her. They said I had no business bumming around the way I did. I wasn't a good influence. Kickboxer. Whatever that was. Writer. You've got to be kidding. Taoist, Zen Buddhist. Too weird to even think about. What kind of future did she think she'd have with a flake like me?

From the beginning, I encouraged Lyn to take chances with her painting when the Harrises discouraged her. Lyn earned several hundred dollars a year from her art while still in high school. The day she graduated, her father told her she'd never make a living from painting and forced her to take a full-time summer job carrying forty-pound trays of tobacco second shift in a plant at R. J. Reynolds Tobacco Company, where Mr. Harris worked as an engineer. "To show you what the real world is like," he said.

The unstated declaration was that this would keep Lyn away from me. The Harrises didn't know that I met Lyn each morning at one o'clock in the plant's parking lot when she got off work. Her ears ringing from machine noise, her skin and fingernails and cilia caked with tobacco dirt, she often laid her head on my shoulder and wept black tobacco tears.

There was so much friction between the Harrises and me that they told Lyn they didn't want me in their house and not to feed me if I came over to see her. "We don't have food in our house for that boy," Lyn's mother said right to my face when they got home from church early one morning and found me in their kitchen eating a tomato sandwich.

To my way of thinking, Lyn has been abused by the Harrises just about her whole life. I know they haven't meant to, but the damage has been done. I feel that's the major reason she's paralyzed when it comes to pursuing her art or much of anything else. I've come to believe that's why she quit college, too— the fear of failure she learned from her parents. I'm glad Daddy didn't heap any of that baggage on me and I haven't been shy about letting Lyn know that this is the way I feel.

"We pretty much knew what your father's situation was," I now tell her. "We knew he needed a bypass. We really don't know with Daddy."

Besides, Lyn adores my father and talks with him much more easily than I ever have. And more readily than she does with me. She even continued to talk with Daddy when she wouldn't have anything to do with me after she and I were divorced.

"He's okay," she says, not dismissively, just convinced. "The kids are having a great time. If anything happens, if there's any kind of emergency, give me a call. Otherwise, we'll see you sometime Sunday."

*   *   *

Saturday morning. "With winds in advance of one hundred miles per hour, Hugo has become a category two hurricane," the announcer reports. "Make no mistake about it," he proclaims, eyes aflame, "this is a major storm."

From the end of the bed, I toss Daddy his favorite summer pajamas, the short ones with tan and brown stripes. I tug and stretch and pull, but his feet are so swollen that I can't get his slippers on.

Still, Daddy looks better today: stabilized and fairly secure. His color remains deep, almost glowing. The heart monitor reads 76. Yes. Much better.

"Dave, I appreciate you bringin' these things by," he tells me, "but I hadn't been able to wear these pajamas for years."

Has it really been so long since I've seen Daddy in PJs? Is he really that much rounder? Sitting behind him on the window ledge, I watch his Adam's apple move as he drinks the pint of skim milk that was brought with his breakfast of powdered eggs and apple slices. Even with this awful food, he's got a healthy appetite, another favorable sign. He places the empty carton on his tray. "My back's sore," he says.

It's my turn to try to comfort him.

I stand above Daddy and gently massage his upper back and shoulders, probably for the first time ever. I'm surprised by the thickness of his trapezius muscles and the softness of his skin.

I call Carol about nine P.M, feeling lucky to catch her home during Labor Day weekend. She asks why I didn't phone earlier. "You know Daddy," I explain, "always wanting to shield us from everything."

In the background, I hear the weather guy on her TV. "Hugo's been upgraded to a category four storm," he excitedly proclaims, not hiding his glee. "Jamaica needs to get ready for a real ride. This is the hurricane of the century." Billions of dollars in property damage, thousands homeless, hundreds dead—now, here's a reason to celebrate.

Monday morning, Labor Day. Lyn and the kids got in from the beach late last night. She started work today, saying she'll visit Daddy on her break, after his catheterization. This morning, he's still quiet, but different: holding himself with confidence, having been regularly reassured by docs, nurses, Carol, me.

Like most of the salaried world, Carol has the holiday off. With relief that Daddy's doing the right thing, we cheer him off for his procedure. He'll be fully conscious the whole time, we're told, and will be back in CCU about ten. I ask Carol if she'd like breakfast. We drive to a waffle place down the street. When we come back about nine-fifteen, a nurse says she's been looking for us. "Your father had some trouble. He's asking for you."

My legs go weak, but I run toward his cubicle. Ten feet away, I slow to a walk and force myself to look calm. He's cranked up in bed again, transparent plastic draped loosely about his head and torso; a thin, clear hose in each nostril; fat tubing exiting the shroud. A wet sucking sound fills the room. I've never seen an oxygen tent, but I'm pretty sure that's what this is. I remember Daddy telling Carol and me about the one they put our mother under, the day she died, in this same hospital.

I ask Daddy how he's doing. He looks almost okay, a little tired and scared. "Better than I was an hour ago," he says, his voice careful, intimate, and amazed. Some of the deep emptiness is back in his eyes, and something else is there, too, something I can't name. For a moment, I can't watch anymore; I look up at the TV: Hugo swirls monochromatically. I don't want to see this, either.

I take a seat on the windowsill and stare out at a slice of blue sky. For so many of my years, I've been able to do whatever was necessary, could get the things I've wanted and needed; I have believed that I am empowered, have believed that because I am kind and fair, the universe takes care of me and those I love. I concentrate hard on the sliver of sky, and on the building's brick as it burns with morning sun, as if they can help me get what I want now.

Carol stands to Daddy's left and holds his hand. She, too, looks into the distance, looks off, steady. A handsome guy not much older than me comes in, shakes my hand and Carol's and Daddy's, and introduces himself as "Steve Mills, the cardio-thoracic surgeon who supervised your cath."

Steve Mills asks me, "What do you do for a living?"

"I write sometimes," I say. "For magazines."

"Can you do that here?" he says, meaning Winston-Salem.

"Anywhere there's a post office . . . I hope." I try to laugh. The noise that comes out is chalk-dry and breaks like twigs underfoot.

Steve Mills clears his throat and looks at my father. And right then, I get the answer to one of those questions all of us wonder about, although I'm certain we never want to know the answer. How would the doctor tell you that you were dying? That you might die this very day?

He did it in this way: He looked terse, regretful, understanding, sympathetic, yet removed. It's something he did not want to do, something he'd rather put off, like having to fire someone from a job, remove a person from a position, and he wanted very much to seem like one of us, without allowing himself to get so close as to go mad with our lives. It's exactly the way I envisioned it would be, but never expected to hear. It's all you could ask from a stranger.

"Mr. Miller," he said without having to look at a chart, "there are three major vessels that supply blood to your heart. Two of them are completely blocked with plaque, the third is ninety-five percent closed. And your heart muscle isn't working well. The left chamber is enlarged and isn't contracting properly. It can't pump blood. The right chamber isn't functioning well, either. This is recent damage. Sometimes the heart muscle gets stunned. It's possible it could recover. I can't say. This is one of those times we just don't know what to do. Our technology's not very good in this area. We have several options—but no matter what we try, there's a slim chance for success. Do you understand what I'm saying?"

"You're sayin' I'm between a rock and a hard place."

"That's about it," said Dr. Mills.

And I moved to Daddy's side. And I held my father's hand and I stroked his hair, things I had not done since I was twelve years old.

Since my mother's death, and the way I shut down in reaction to it, Daddy has done his very best to shield me from every painful thing that he could. This time, though, he doesn't need to spend his time worrying about me. By the time the cardiologist leaves the room and Carol says she's going to the bathroom (for an unobserved cry, I guess), I've decided that no matter what, I'm going to stay right with this, I'm not going to look the other way, it's not fair to Daddy to do anything less.

For minutes, I work toward the courage to tell him what I've believed I'd have all the time in the world to say. "You and I never tell each other how we feel," I start, my voice maybe half steady. "But I think I should say this now—you've been the best father I could ever imagine having had."

Then: My throat shuts tight. I can't utter one more word. Daddy starts to cry, as do I. He reaches to take me in his arms and to kiss me on the lips, and I him. We're stopped by the plastic tent. "I've got things to tell you, too, son," he says in the near-voice. "But I just can't do it right now."

You know what happens next, but I'm going to show you some of it anyway.

Lyn takes off from work and comes to see Daddy, as do her parents. "Hey, sweetheart," Daddy says as Lyn steps into the room. She sits beside him and holds his hand.

I ask my father if he'd like Johanna and Isaac to visit. He says we'll have to see how it goes. I stay close to Daddy, but we talk only about the hurricane and about other things that don't much matter.

Early afternoon, I'm alone with him as a nurse comes to check his pulse and the flow of medications from his I.V. As she busies herself, he closes his eyes for a long moment. When he opens them, he asks the nurse for nitroglycerin.

"Have you had pain?" she says, turning her eyes to the monitor. I look at the monitor and I look at her. Daddy's pulse is 78. Everything looks fine to me.

"You're getting nitro in your I.V.," says the nurse. "That's what this plastic bag is. Are you having pain right now?"

Daddy closes his eyes again. "I breathe better when I'm sittin' up," he says. "I'm havin' some trouble breathin'. Will you put me up a little bit more?"

The nurse looks at him, long, and looks at the monitor.

"I don't want to give you a hard time," says my father, "but if you don't put me up, I'm gonna climb out of this bed." Even now, Daddy's the foreman, trying to take care of everything. As always, wanting to make everything all right.

Trying not to appear hurried, but without a word, the nurse leaves the cubicle. She quickly returns with a young dark-haired man in green scrubs, maybe a resident, who doesn't say anything, just looks at the monitor. I move over beside Daddy and take his hand. The man in green puts Daddy down flat. Daddy closes his eyes and bears down so tight on his lips that they go white; he shakes his head, big and slow, from side to side. I grit my teeth. Two more people enter the cubicle and hasten to Daddy's side. There's a hand gentle at the inside of my forearm, near the elbow. "We need you to leave now," comes a woman's voice, soft and level. She pulls the curtain closed behind me.

It's five interminable hours before they let me in with Daddy. Carol and Lyn and I are eventually taken to a waiting room, where we're told he's had a major myocardial infarction, and probably a stroke, that he's very near death. We take this all in real smooth, like swimming underwater in a deep, black pool.

There's no way I could be prepared for what I find when I'm finally allowed into his space. When the plastic curtain is pulled back, Daddy has been replaced by a giant orange frog that looks a little like my father. Sure, this frog has a birthmark on its neck in the same place as my father's; it has his thin lips, too, and a gold-edged tooth way in the back like

Daddy. And it even has the little cut under the chin
Daddy got this morning when he sat on the end of
the bed and shaved without a mirror, as well as the
whiskers he missed, the ones that have gotten long
from not having shaved all weekend. But this isn't my
father.

The frog's head has been thrown back at a horri-
bly contorted angle. Its neck is grotesquely edema-
tous, the right eye closed, the cornea of the
unseeing left shudders electrically. Its mouth is as
slack as a worn-out sock. A clear tube disappears
under the sheets; one from the nose bears an inter-
mittent stream of black blood. The smell that fills
this space has a presence, and the presence is more
powerful than any other phenomenon in the room.
Indeed, it is the most powerful (most real) thing
I've ever been around. Nothing else has even come
close.

I'm so in awe that it's days, weeks, months before I
get pissed off, or even know what to get pissed off
about. When I do, I'm not angry with the docs,
nurses, et al., who put in their very best efforts to
keep Daddy alive. But my father was used as an ex-
periment, as a teaching aid. There were times when a
hive of fifteen or so people swarmed about his
deathbed; altogether, as many as forty strangers were
around my father when his own immediate family
wasn't allowed to be with him. I'm angry that I was
disconnected from Daddy at a time of terrible intimacy, that I was rushed from his side, when surely no
one had any right, legal or otherwise, to do so. When

I get the bill from the hospital, there are ten long indecipherable pages of chemicals that were shot through his system during those last few hours. I'm fucking mad that Daddy was unintentionally tortured in this way. And what I'd like to do is kick the gonads off of the system that teaches people to treat other living, breathing human beings as mechanistically as they do. And maybe I'd like to snatch the Big Ancient White Cat Himself off His mountain, drag Him down by His long scraggly white-ass beard and knock the Holy Shit out of Him for designing it this way, or letting it be this way, or for not telling us why, or just for something. Maybe all I really want to do is just ask Him what the fuck He thinks He's doing.

Or maybe it's just the old concept of Mr. White-Beard that I'd like to snatch from the mountain.

Anyway, I stay with Daddy as long as they let me and I hold his hand and talk with him. His fingers constantly tremble, but when I tell him that I love him, he seems to press his middle finger into the heart of my palm. Carol doesn't go in to see him, and I think this is probably best. She says she can't bear it, and that she wants to remember him the way he was. The waiting room fills with people, including his brother from Charlotte, his sister from D.C., and a number of longtime friends. I'm the only one who sees Daddy during those last hours.

Daddy lets the world out of his lungs the next morning, September 6, 1989, at 8:25 A.M., when his heart finally gives out. At the funeral on Friday, in the casket, Daddy looks more like himself than he did in the hospital those last hours. Carol tugs Daddy's gold watch from his wrist and places it on mine. It's an Elgin, given to him just a few months ago for forty years of service with the corrugated box company. On the band, there's a two-point diamond that's connected to a company logo. This is the first time I've even looked at a watch since I threw mine in the Ohio.

Daddy is buried beside his mother and his father, at a cemetery right around the corner and down the hill, a half mile or so from their house, where Lyn and the kids and I will be living for a while. Talk about upsetting. If it weren't for all the trees in between, Lyn and I could look out of our bedroom window and straight across at everybody's graves.

Within hours after Daddy is in the ground, Lyn and her parents and the kids and I drive to Raleigh, where her brother is to be married the next day.

I don't want to go to Scott's wedding, but don't need to stay home, either. As everyone else talks, I sit at the backseat window pretty much watching nothing until the sun sets, bruising the sky. As soon as we get to Raleigh, we drive to a restaurant named The Plantation, where we're to meet the wedding party for dinner. A REMINDER OF GENTLER TIMES IN THE OLD SOUTH, reads the sign beside the road.

A one-fourth-mile horseshoe-shaped drive lined with tall loblolly pines dripping with Spanish moss leads to the restaurant; giant, glossy-leaved magnolias surround the building itself, an ersatz rendering of an Atlanta cotton plantation. Although magnolias typically flower only in the spring, the trees are rich with white blossoms. The weird weather must have something to do with it.

Inside, the walls are covered with pink and green floral wallpaper and mildewed portraits of Southern gentry. A hundred or more people dressed in suits and ties and bright, flowing party dresses are seated at long banquet tables before steaming platters of fried chicken and biscuits, country ham and redeye gravy, ceramic bowls of mashed potatoes and milk gravy, pintos cooked in pig fat, potato salad, fried okra and squash, sweating pitchers of sweetened iced tea. Southern cooking. The very foods that clogged my father's arteries.

Folks laugh and tell stories in slow musical melodies while sucking on R. J. Reynolds cigarettes, the same brands Daddy smoked for forty-five years. R. J. Reynolds Tobacco Company, Winston-Salem's homegrown conglomerate. As a child, I remember waking every morning with the intoxicatingly sweet smell of cured tobacco from the RJR plants hanging in the air. I want to beat hell out of every cocksucker who ever worked in any way for the fucking tobacco industry.

I walk through the room, out the back door, and around the building. It's a muggy, windless night. The air smells of car exhaust. I listen to the electric sound of cicadas, stick my face deep in magnolia blossoms, even smear the rubbery flowers all over my face, but can't get that other smell, the one in Daddy's cubicle, out of my nose.

Suddenly Lyn is in front of me. She says: What are you doing? You could come back inside with everybody else, she says. I asked you if you wanted to stay home, she tells me.

I turn away. There's a streetlamp a ways off and the ground around it has a greenish glow. I walk toward the light.

The lamp illuminates a children's playground. A seesaw, sandbox, teeter-totter, a big set of swings. I take a seat on the middle swing, lay my head way back, and try to look through the dull orange glow of city lights, searching for shapes in the clouds. I don't see any.

It's not at all like Hollywood, I think. You have memories, but not the big stuff, the events. You remember how, when you were little, he liked to drive in the rain and that he packed everybody in the car to head downtown in summer storms; how he blew his nose, the sound not so much of his voice as of his cough, the arc of his fingernails, the way he slurped his milk. Nothing dramatic.

And you start finding him in almost every personal gesture you thought was your own. Even the way I sign my name is like Daddy's. In junior high, I worked for hours to emulate his handwriting, not only so I could forge his name on my report card when I failed classes, but because his signature was so graceful, so very beautiful.

When I was small, maybe five or six, Daddy'd put me on the big swings and I'd get dizzy, feel sick; I'd be terrified. I'd cry and cry, really wail. Now I plant my feet in the sand and push back hard, kick my legs way up. I watch pines whisk past, then sand, then grass, pines, sand, grass. I go up and up. Pushing, pumping.

It's the only thing that makes any sense at all. Swinging on the big swings. Swinging hard. Just kick those legs up and pump for the sky.

SECTION III

In His Voice

Eighteen

_____

M_y Dinner with Ali" is run the Sunday after
Scott's wedding. I call Mrs. Clay to be sure she sees
the story. "Couldn't miss it," she tells me. "Everybody's been bringing me copies. My niece just read
me the whole thing. It's so long, but so good. Sweet,
so sweet."

The _Courier-Journal_ editor phones from his home,
offering congratulations for what he claims will be
the beginning of an "illustrious career," and saying
that the in-house response has been considerable.
"People in other departments have been giving me
'Attaboys' for publishing such a fine, fine piece," he
says.

I wish I could feel good about these reactions, but I
just don't feel much of anything. It's all I can do to
tread water.

The next afternoon, I'm asleep on the sofa when the phone rings once again. It's an editor of a sports magazine. "Saw your story in the Louisville paper," he says. "We've never run reprints, but I want to make an exception. I can offer fifteen hundred dollars for the piece. If you take it to a big magazine, you'll get more for it, but I'll honor the writing."

Here it is. Finally. Some kind of success. At a time when I have no possibility of sharing it with Daddy. Although he didn't read ten books in his life, Daddy would've loved to see my work. The only thing of mine he ever read, however, was that little article in *Sports Illustrated.* I never showed him other stories, wanting to wait until I could bring them to him in print. I thought it was important for him to see that somebody besides family actually thought that I was doing good work. It completely sucks that it's too late now.

Ten days after Daddy's death, with 150-mile-per-hour winds and amid orgasmic oratory from weather announcers ("Look at the symmetry. Watch this rotation. We won't see the likes of this storm again for a long, long time"), category five Hugo slams the South Carolina coastline, then slashes inland and up the coast, tearing through Winston-Salem and the rest of western North Carolina with 75mph gusts and windstorms, before finally covering the fierce and sucking sun long enough to bring inches and inches of rain to Kentucky and the parched and cracked Midwest. A meteorologist interviewed on NPR says that if global warming goes uncurbed, by the middle of the next century we can expect super-hurricanes with 300-mile-per-hour winds. In my grandmother's yard, during Hugo's churning passage, two big old cedars are ripped up by their roots and we're shocked from four A.M. sleep when a scorching bolt of lightning shreds the air right overhead and strikes Daddy's grave.

Or at least that's what I see and feel in my sleep before I jump from bed, shaking and screaming and weeping, drenched with sweat. Lyn gets up, too, and hugs me to her chest and rubs my back, slow and gentle, yet I can't go back to sleep. When she drops away to sleep, I get up, dry off with a towel, pour a glass of grape juice, and, although I think about putting on a CD and listening to it through headphones, I watch some dumb forties musical and listen to the wind moan and snarl until the sun rises.

Since Daddy's death, for the first time as an adult, I've stopped listening to music. For years, I've enjoyed—even felt enriched and stimulated by—elegiac music. Some of my all-time favorite pieces have been Copland's "Our Town" and Barber's "Adagio for Strings." But that's when my father was alive. And although I often thought about my own mortality and the nature of mortality itself, it was with the romance of distance, like watching my shadow beside me as I walked. Now music with edge, with substance, hurts beyond bearing; anything playful is fat with false promise. About the only noise I can handle is no noise at all. Which makes me Mr. Jokes and Laughs around Lyn and the kids.

As an adult, I've not seen much reason to honor the skeletonized hand of the past. But now I find myself wearing Daddy's watch, his tennis shoes, his athletic socks, even the tan-striped pajamas I brought him in the hospital. And I stare at his grandkids as if their skin might crack open at any moment: For the first time, I see a striking resemblance between Isaac and Daddy—the spiky fineness of hair, the round face, the tenderness in both their eyes, even the birthmarks high on the backs of their necks. And Johanna favors my mother so much that they could've been twins. "It hurt Daddy every time he looked at her," Carol tells me. "He loved being around her, but he just didn't think he could tell you the way he felt."

What changes I'm going through. Last Friday, there I was, standing in front of a bank teller, depositing an insurance voucher for one hundred thousand dollars (and my $400 check from the *Courier-Journal*), more money than I thought I'd ever see at one time in my whole life.

"God, I've never had a check like this," the cute, soft-tressed teller enviously exclaimed. "God, it must feel good to cash a check like this."

I just wanted to cry. That morning, I'd already gone by the corrugated box plant, to return Daddy's Taurus and talk with Mr. Sloane, the plant manager. It's all I could do to force myself to accept the company insurance check when Mr. Sloane handed it to me. I wanted to tear the cursed thing up right on the spot and be done with it.

But there's more on the way. Carol and I'll divide

the money from the sale of Daddy's house. With the insurance, that'll be enough to put a down payment on another house, pay off debts, and generally solve just about all money woes Lyn and I have, at least for a while. And I feel like snake shit about the whole thing.

What to make of this? One thing for sure—interconnectedness ain't all smiley, smiley, let's come together, drink a Coke, pet a puppy, and sing Barry Manilow songs.

Serendipity. Isn't that a real interesting concept, particularly considering what appear to be the realities. I feel somewhat secure saying only maybe two things in this world. One: We don't know a damn thing (no one has known and we shall not know). Two: Everything we see in the universe, from subatomic to cosmic, is eating someone, and is being eaten by someone else. That's some pretty scary stuff. And yet, we're such a hopeful species. How amazing.

Lately, my dreams haven't been nearly as frightening as all this real life. Every night, every dream, it's been about Daddy. Yet none of them have been horrific, as they were when my mother and Mandy and my grandfather and grandmother died. Then, whoever had passed on would appear as a walking, talking corpse—the longer since the time of death, the greater the decomposition. Dreams about Daddy have been sort of comforting. Except for the one last night, he hasn't been dead in any of them. And that one feels as much like a visitation as a dream, anyway. It went kind of like this: I'm down in the basement of my grandparents' house, feeding Dallas or doing laundry or something. I look up and there he is, coming right through the wall. He glides out and toward me, his face flat, without expression, but not particularly sad. He stops about five feet away.

I just wanted to say good-bye, he tells me.

I reach for him, but he's already less, sliding back to the wall, then less still, retreating, his face remaining expressionless and now transparent, less than shadow, then gone, his atoms having merged, again with those of the wall.

Maybe the reason there's a kind of solace in these dreams is that I don't feel any guilt in Daddy's death. Mostly because of what I told him in those last hours, I'm sure, and probably because through his death I've grown some. At the very moment he died, I felt the metamorphosis take place: Suddenly my father was in me; my movements became his movements, his movements were mine. The whole situation, profound though it is, feels plain goddamn awful.

And yet there's this odd, undeniable, personal providence about it all. If Daddy hadn't died, I certainly would not have had the opportunity to pursue a writing career in the way that this money allows. Stranger still, I'd have a lot less story to tell you. Now, what am I supposed to make of all that?

Nineteen

Moving from one life and into another.

With everything going on, it's weeks before Lyn gets her suitcases unpacked. Then another big storm whips through, flooding the basement and ruining most of the stuff in the boxes we had shipped from Louisville.

The house in Kentucky sells for about what we paid for it and Lyn and I buy a place built the same year Daddy was born, 1930. Even though it costs more than the Louisville house, it's not nearly as nice. Housing isn't as affordable in Winston-Salem as in the Louisville area and almost every home here is traditional or neo-traditional—those horrible "modern" studies in cultural hypertrophy, the ones where they rip the trees from the land, and sometimes even the sod itself, and thrust multistoried, almost windowless brick boxes up against the sky—the ones Lyn calls mausoleums.

The old cottage we buy isn't nearly so bad as all that, but it's not our ideal, either. On the good side, it has big bright rooms, an oddity in Winston, and a converted attic that I'll use for an office. At the closing, Lyn has me promise not to move again before 1994. "Thirteen times in twelve years is enough," she says.

Even before "My Dinner with Ali" is scheduled by the editor at the sports magazine, the Sunday Magazine Editors Association judges it to be the Best Essay published in the U.S. in 1989. The *Courier-Journal* sends me a plaque and I'm invited to a dinner in some city in Iowa or someplace that no one will pay for me to attend. Then the photo editor from the sports magazine calls to ask if Ali might sit for a portrait. I tell him that Ali's sort of a recluse, he doesn't do that anymore. "Ask if he'll let us take a few pictures of his hands," says the editor. "Just his hands."

I say I can't promise anything but I'll try. I call the farm, Ali answers the phone. "You ain't no writer," he says, when I get up the nerve to tell him why I've called. "They just usin' you."

"I've wanted to write for years. Like you, when you threw your gold medal off the bridge, I threw my beeper in the river and quit my job so I could write."

"I never did that," he says.

"Did what?" I ask.

"Never threw my medal off no bridge. Just lost it, that's all."

"You serious?"

"*Maannn*, that's a story I made up. I know what it takes to sell a story."

"What matters," I say, "is the ways you influenced me. What matters is I did it because I thought you had."

"Shoulda wrote about me when I wanted people writin'. I'm gold, I know I'm gold. People come around me thinkin' they're slick."

"I'm different," I tell him. "I wouldn't do anything to hurt you."

"There ain't no such thing as different," he says, which stops me cold. "They always tryin' to use my friends like you. How much they pay you?"

I tell him. Now it's his turn to be quiet. Surely he's surprised by how little I'll get.

"I wouldn't do anything that would hurt you," I say. "Your mother loved the story. Said it was the best ever about the family."

"My mother don't have nothin' to say about what I do."

"There's not enough money in the world for me to hurt you. I don't mean to upset you."

I wait for him to say something, but he doesn't. I stammer around a little, not saying anything that makes much sense, but not knowing what to do. Eventually, I tell him I hope to see him sometime soon and I hang up, doubting that Ali had a clue who he was talking to. On the phone, there's simply no way he knew. He probably didn't even know who I was last time, when he invited me up to Berrien

Springs. It doesn't much matter. I feel so terrible about his reaction that I don't know if I ever want to write another word about him, or anyone else. At least about anyone who isn't a fictional character.

Within a couple weeks, I get the $1,500, the biggest paycheck I've ever had for anything. *Sport* magazine publishes "My Dinner with Ali" in its next issue. Instead of photographs, it's run with pen-and-ink drawings that Lyn's work would've dramatically skunked. I tried to get her to contribute illustrations. I'm sure the magazine would've used them. I think it would've been fun to work with her and she would've been paid at least $500. But she said she'd be afraid to try and that no matter what she did, I wouldn't be satisfied with it. It's really too bad she feels this way.

A month or so later the piece is nominated for a Maggie award; my editor says that Maggies are the Pulitzer Prizes of magazine awards. The interest in "My Dinner with Ali" continues: I'm invited to an awards banquet in upstate New York, where I'll be named Writer of the Year by the American Association for the Improvement of Boxing. The Detroit *Free Press* magazine wants to run the piece, too, as does my hometown paper, the Winston-Salem *Journal.* And I find out that a martial arts rag in England has already published it, without my permission and without paying me a single quid. I call a solicitor in London, who tells me that I can sue if I want but that it won't get me anywhere.

* * *

In late October, I hear on the radio that Sugar Ray Leonard has signed to fight Roberto Duran for the third time. Other than Ali, Leonard's the only boxer I've ever cared about watching. Back in '76, when I first saw him, I was impressed with his Ali-like, hands-dropping flashiness. But unlike Ali, Leonard was no force of nature. Those cutesy sailor suits, his smarmy little cherubic wink and smile. I had a robust enough ego to fully believe that, if given the chance, I could whup Ray Leonard. I was faster than him and moved better, I thought. Of course, that was before I realized I wasn't half as good as I imagined. And it was before I had seen him fight with great balls and beauty time and again. Now the 1989 version of me thinks I can write about Leonard in a way that no one else has. For years I've wanted to develop a Zen boxing piece, and Ray Leonard is perfect for what I have in mind.

I pick up the phone and call the editor at *Sport*. "Okay, I agree with you," he says. "We need to do something for this fight. You want to be a writer. You want to write about boxing. I'll give you the chance. Give me two thousand words, and I'll pay the same money we paid for the Ali story. But I need the piece quick. Have it here in two weeks."

This is kind of a big deal. My first-ever real assignment in which someone sends me out to interview somebody about something. For a magazine with millions of readers each month. A piece about the Zen of boxing. If I can write about swimming with the stream, I can live it.

I call directory assistance in Bethesda, Maryland,
ask the number for Mike Trainer, Leonard's longtime
attorney, and give his office a call, setting up a meeting for next week at Leonard's gym in Palmer Park,
Maryland.

Twenty

Ray Leonard Road in Palmer Park. A young, skinny, long-legged dog trots up the street between a fading, wine-colored velveteen sofa and a rusted-out, mustard-yellow washing machine, both of which have been decorated with flashing Christmas lights. The dirt-brown hound crosses the road, turns its head in my direction. It grins supplicatingly, then ambles up a knoll to lift its leg to a short white picket fence that surrounds two sides of a less than one-thousand-square-foot wooden cottage that has been painted red, white, and blue.

"That's it," says the wealthiest athlete we've yet had. "That's the one I grew up in."

We're sitting in Leonard's champagne-colored Mercedes. "You know what I wanted when I was a kid?" he says. "I wanted to be a Boy Scout. We couldn't afford the uniforms, the fees. I went to the Goodwill Thrift Shop and they had a uniform. I bought it for fifty cents and wore it everywhere I went. And I was proud. I wore that uniform and told everybody I was a Boy Scout. I wore it so proud."

Today, Leonard's sporting a purple double-breasted jacket, a bone-white silk shirt, a pair of knife-creased soft gold slacks, and purple Chinese-style slippers hand-embroidered with red and gold stitchery. This single outfit must have cost as much as his father made in several months when the family was living on this corner.

I talk with Ray about greatness. "Do you want to become a great man?" I ask, wondering (at least for the magazine's purposes) why he hasn't stayed retired.

"Man," he says, "I'm just a fighter. That's all. If you want to know about greatness, watch Muhammad Ali. Watch people around Ali. If you put him in a hall of people with Castro and Gorbachev," he says, "everybody'd flock to Ali. That's greatness."

Twenty-one

I occasionally have dreams in which old Ali is still fighting. Sometimes, in these dreams, his body is classically Greek and his fists explode into blurs. More often, he's not at all well.

In the dreams, I'm never actually at the fight; I'm watching TV or listening to the radio, the way I did in Daddy's house.

Last night, Ali was facing George Foreman. I was staring down on the ring as if from heaven. At the bell for Round One, Ali tosses a jab that's more a push than a punch. Foreman backs Ali to the ropes and Ali covers up. Like in the first Norton fight, Ali's skin looks green under God's television lights; adipose tissue hangs in folds from his chest and hips. He's too slow to score with his punches; Foreman never connects, either. Soon both old warriors recognize the futility. They break and go to their corners, but quickly return to the center of the ring with their stools, on which they sit and begin a debate about Islam and Christianity. The referee, at first, is the Old Cat Himself and then the ref becomes my father, who's sick and dying.

Old Mr. White-Beard has ridden His whirlwind back to His mountaintop, leaving Ali and Foreman and my dad and me and all of us to sort this out, alone and in pain. My father is the best man I have known; he spent his whole life going out of his way to avoid hurting anyone. He doesn't deserve the pain and doesn't deserve to be alone. I stand from my seat on the sofa in his house and prepare to jump into the TV screen. I don't want to look down on this anymore. I've got to save my father, and save Ali and save all of us.

"I'm young and handsome and fast and pretty and can't possibly be beat," Ali said so many decades before. The irony's too fucking obvious. *Most times* it's too obvious. Every high-school kid in love knows about irony. Wouldn't one simple unironical moment, every once in a while, when deserved, be more meaningful than the trillion or so ironies we could see every day, if we looked for them?

Daddy is lying on his hospital bed and is shaking his head. He's carefully saved money from his small salary while raising two kids by himself; he's ready to retire and enjoy himself, but here he is: He can't speak but his head is moving from side to side and his lips are scrunched up tight and I know he doesn't want to die.

I jump straight into the TV screen. Right into the lines of blue light.

But then I wake. As usual, without getting to do anything about anything. Other than going upstairs to write about it.

I labor over this story for a couple hours. Just when I get it down on paper and it reads as if it makes some kind of sense, my own young son comes upstairs and gives me a hug and tells me good morning.

Twenty-two

The five-thousand-room Mirage Hotel and Casino is celebrating its grand opening. Directly across from the main entrance, a fifty-six-foot-high man-made waterfall suddenly rumbles and hisses and spits piña-colada-scented, flaming natural gas thirty feet into the air. On Las Vegas Boulevard, dozens of cars stop to watch the "volcano." A gaping, yelling crowd of hundreds leans against guardrails on the sidewalks. A group of twenty Tibetan Buddhists, in orange robes and leather sandals, stands in seeming serenity near the street. Their shaved pates gleam with the re-flected light of the flames.

Just inside the hotel, a pair of near-life-sized brass mermaids sprawl in a lascivious pose atop marble platforms, boldly thrusting shining bare breasts into the faces of passersby. A bone-thin white-haired woman in her seventies sits on one of the platforms, watching her feet. Two Middle Eastern men in their late forties take turns at the other statue, having their photographs taken pretending to suckle slightly post-adolescent nipples.

Behind the registration desk, there's a blue-watered aquarium rich with twisting sharks and to the left of the main casino, a white, glass-enclosed room in which white Bengal tigers prowl and shit and sleep. At feeding times, the animals are removed from public display.

These meretriciously American visual stimuli were designed by Steve Wynn, the owner of the Mirage. The movie-handsome Wynn has rain-forest-thick black hair, sun-bronzed skin, snapping black eyes, and *retinitis pigmentosa* that will cause his field of vision to narrow until he goes blind.

I'm at the Mirage as *Sport* magazine's representative for the Leonard-Duran fight. My piece came out well; a show on a sports TV network built a half-hour Leonard interview around the quotes and ideas in my story. A ringside seat and picking up my expenses for the trip—these are the ways my editor rewards me. What I care about more than Leonard, Duran, my ringside seat, the Mirage, Steve Wynn, Las Vegas, or the Zen of pugilism is that Ali will make an appearance at the fight.

I get to Vegas a couple days before the bout. After unpacking my suitcase, I open the curtains to look out at the naked sky. On the ledge ten feet below sits a large bird. A hawk!

The next morning, the bird is still there. Unmoving. Dead.

Hot-air balloons dyed in rainbow colors drift over the mountains to the north. I stay in the room all morning, reading and ordering room service, doing push-ups and feeling not quite ready to go out in the world. Daddy's death keeps hitting me harder than any fist ever could. During the days, I've been having chest pains, and at night, I still dream about him, every single dream. I turn on the radio beside the bed, not having listened to the airwaves since he died, doubting that I'll find a station that's even remotely listenable. I mean, Jesus, this is Vegas. The home of Wayne Newton, Kenny Rogers, and Frank Sinatra, Jr. But there it is. Sort of like stumbling across an ancient Taoist scroll in the bargain bin at the five and dime—a terrific Van Morrison tune I haven't heard before: "I Forgot that Love Existed." I catch the song right at the beginning. When it's over, I have to admit that I feel a little better. In my grief and bereavement over Daddy, yes, I have forgotten. These past months, life has felt even more evanescent than ever. Life isn't who we are. It's on us, it's a garment we wear. We wear our lives as raincoats.

How weird. Is this insight? Do we ever know what's going on? That which is regarded as insight, as "high" art and "serious" understanding, may often be mostly a by-product of good ole homegrown asswhupping grief and/or depression. What can we know of reality, anyway? Would a father who just learned that his teenage daughter has been squashed

dead by a drunk driver on this gorgeous Sunday afternoon see the lake behind his house the same way
as the freshly engaged couple who have decided to
make an offer to buy a two-bedroom cottage on the
other side of the lake?

Needing to get out of the room, to finally move
around some and quit thinking about all this stuff, I
go down to the casino and right off spot a familiar
face. "Lonnie," I call as she walks past, heading for
the penthouse elevator. "Lonnie Ali," I say as she
turns around. "I hope you remember me. I'm Davis
Miller."

"Oh, Davy. Sure I remember you. I was just going
up to the room. Come on with me. Muhammad'll be
glad to see you."

"Muhammad, you have a visitor," Lonnie says as
she opens the door to the top-floor suite. "It's Davy."

Yeah, I like it. I really do like being called Davy.
Going through life with a first name that's also a last
name makes you feel you have something to live up
to; a nickname like Davy allows me to dress down a
bit.

Ali is sitting on a small white sofa near full-length
windows that overlook the east side of town. He's
wearing a pair of dark pinstripe slacks and a white V-
neck T-shirt that has a couple nickel-sized holes in it,
one of which reveals whorls of thin white hair on the
left side of his chest. He's munching a big muffin that
looks small in his fist. He's the heaviest I've seen him.

I'd guess he's at about 265. "My man," he says. "How's Loovul?"

I remind him that I don't live in Kentucky anymore. He seems not to take interest; his eyes go dull. He gets up from his seat and walks stiffly to the windows. The label of his white cotton Blue Knight briefs is sticking out of the top of his pants. He motions for me to follow.

"Look at this place," he says, whispering. "This big hotel, this town. It's dust, all dust. Steve Wynn, thinkin' he's some kind of pharaoh, buildin' this big tombstone like it'll make him immortal."

His voice is so volumeless that the words seem to be spoken not by Ali, but by a specter standing in his shadow. "Elvis, Kennedy, Martin Luther King, they all dead. It's all only dust."

We stare down at the sun-bleached town. In the middle distance, just before the edge of the Spring Mountains, a military fighter touches down at an air base. "Go up in an airplane," Ali is saying, his voice rattling with phlegm and ether. "Fly real low, we look like toys. Go high enough and it's like we don't even exist. I've been everywhere in the world, seen everything, had everything a man can have. Don't none of it mean nothin'." His tone is not cynical.

He shuffles awkwardly back to the sofa and drops heavily into his seat. "The only thing that matters is submitting to the will of God," he says. "The only things you've got is what's been given to you."

He gestures for me to join him by patting the cushion to his left. I take a seat. We touch at knees and shoulders. Lonnie is in a chair across from us and beside the TV.

"How you been?" Ali asks.

"I'm okay," I say, "but my dad died a few months ago."

I realize when I say this that I need to talk with Ali and Lonnie about Daddy. For the life of me, I don't know why.

The Champ jerks his head up, surprised.

"My father just died, too," Lonnie says.

Ali looks at me so empathetically you'd almost think we shared the same parentage. "How old was he?" he asks.

"Only fifty-nine. And I thought he was healthy. I thought I'd have lots of time with him. He was both my father and my mother. It's the hardest thing I've ever been through."

"How'd he pass?" Lonnie asks.

"A heart attack?" says Ali.

I nod yes.

"My father, too," Lonnie says in a tone not dissimilar to Daddy's near-voice. And with a note of connection to my loss.

"I'm sorry, Lonnie," I say, nodding.

Ali pats me on the hand. "I know you miss him. When I first won the title, people used to call me up, messin' with me, tell me my father'd been killed. Used to scare me so bad. Life is so, so short. Bible says it's like a vapor."

Ali picks up the TV's remote control from the sofa's armrest and tours the channels.

Lonnie gets up, her eyes tearing a little. "You two visit while I change clothes," she says and leaves the room.

Ali stops on a music network that's playing an old Michael Jackson hit. He turns off the sound; we watch.

"Gandhi," he says, as the Indian spiritualist's gray ghostlike image flashes onto the screen. "Mother Teresa," a few seconds later. He obviously feels a kinship with the faces and their deeds, and wants me to recognize the connection. He intones the names as if they were incantatory.

When the song is over, he switches to a segment of a workout show. Young chesty women stylishly sweat in blue and pink and yellow Easter-egg-color leotards. "They call this exercisin'," Ali says. "This is what it's really about." He places his left hand near his lap and simulates the common male masturbatory technique. "It's hard not to be tempted by this, unless you got somethin' like I got, somethin' holy.

"Haven't messed around with women in almost five years," he says, low and secretive. "The last time, a brother in Saudi Arabia caught me with a woman. Asked, 'Would you do that in front of your mother?' I told him, 'No.' He pointed at me and said, 'You're doin' it in front of Allah.' *Maaann*, that's heavy. Powerful. He scared me. That's when I really began to get serious about livin' for God."

The Champ uses his right arm to reach across the chrome and glass coffee table. "Want to show you somethin'," he says. When I last saw Ali, his left hand trembled. The right one did not; now it does.

He grabs his briefcase, which lies on the floor in front of us. He places it on his knees and opens it slowly, reverentially, as if revealing the contents of the Ark of the Covenant. When I see inside, I'm reminded of Gandhi's possessions at his time of death—eyeglasses, a watch, two pairs of sandals, an eating bowl, a *Bhagavad-gitā*. Ali's briefcase contains thick stacks of yellow, green, and blue Muslim pamphlets, his own eyeglasses, a photo of himself with "Sugar" Ray Robinson on the left and Joe Louis on the right, a Koran, a Bible. He removes a copy of a painting of Jesus, which he holds up, widening his eyes like he used to when challenging an opponent or the press.

"I carry this everywhere I go. It reminds me just how famous I am. If you had your whole life handed back to you right now, and your one goal, from the moment you were born, was to become famous as this man, how would you do it? If somebody told you some nigger boxer from Loovul, Kentucky, would become famous as Jesus Christ, you'd tell 'em, 'You crazy.' But I did it."

I don't expect to run into Jesus at a gas station or on a street corner, but this big-as-Christ talk makes me uncomfortable for Ali. "Did you?" I ask. "Or was it done for you?"

He grins and laughs like my three-year-old caught with a stick of candy he has been asked not to eat. "You got me there," he says. And then he drapes a bear's arm about my shoulders. "I still get arrogant sometimes. You really straightened me out."

Ali growls his growl and bites his lip. Then, with his thumb and index finger, he grabs my right leg just above the knee and sort of pinches it in a rolling, tickling kind of way. Giggling, I knock his hand to the side. This is the first time I think I've laughed since Daddy died. Leave it to Ali to help me feel better. I say: "Did I ever tell you I lost my virginity during the third Norton fight?"

"You serious?"

"Yeah, man. I was at my father's house with my girlfriend. Nobody was home. We're in my bedroom and we've been there for a while. All of a sudden, Daddy opens the back door. We hadn't heard the car drive up. Lyn jumps out of bed and runs bare-ass for the bathroom, clothes in hand. I flip on the TV, hop into a pair of gym shorts, and try to act like I'm absorbed in the fight. Man, I love you, you know I do, but I'll tell you the truth, I couldn't even see what was going on. You didn't matter at all to me right then. Daddy comes into the room and I'm trying so hard to be calm that I'm shaking everywhere, shaking all over, shaking like I've been pureed in a blender. I know he knew exactly what was going on, but he never said a thing."

Ali laughs a long time, stamping his feet on the floor. As he wipes tears from his eyes, he says, "Your father was a good man."

He returns his briefcase to the floor, stands, moves for the bathroom, and when he gets there, slowly takes a starched white shirt from its hanger on the door and slips it on, then struggles a little with the buttons. Without tucking the shirt in his pants, he pulls a royal-red tie over his head that has been pre-knotted, I'm sure, by Lonnie. He looks at me through the mirror and nods slightly, which I take to mean he'd like my help. In this moment, the most talented athlete of the twentieth century looks so eggshell fragile that I find *my* hands shaking a little. I might have imagined performing this service for my dad, had he lived to his seventies. But never for Muhammad Ali.

Ali is so large that I have to stand on my toes to reach over and across the huge expanse of his back to slip the tie under his collar. He tucks his shirt in his slacks without unsnapping or unzipping, then tugs on his jacket. Without being asked, I pick a few motes of white lint from the jacket's dark surface and help him straighten his tie. He grabs cookies and an apple from the glass dining table and points to his briefcase. I pick it up. We head for the door.

I shout down the hall, saying good-bye to Lonnie. "It's good to see you, Davy," she yells.

In the elevator, Ali leans to me and whispers, "All these people gamblin'. It's important to come to people where they are. Watch how people react."

When we reach the ground floor, he crams cookies in his jacket pocket, pushing the flap halfway down inside, then places the apple core in an ashtray, takes his briefcase from my hand, and, as the elevator door opens, clucks his tongue across the roof of his mouth.

The sound is repeated from about twenty feet away. Within a few seconds, a face appears in the doorway. It's Howard Bingham, Ali's personal photographer and best friend for nearly thirty years. Bingham looks basically the way I recall from the seventies: angular, balding, bearded, and a little hang-jawed like the old MGM cartoon character Droopy. No one—not wives, not children, not even his mother—has been closer to Ali than Bingham.

I introduce myself to Bingham and we walk from the elevator, Ali in the lead; Bingham follows me. We don't get more than fifteen steps before a crowd of probably a hundred people surrounds us, wanting to touch Ali or shake his hand. Cameras appear from women's purses, as do pens and scraps of paper. "Do the shuffle, Champ," an older man shouts.

Ali hands me his briefcase, gets up on his toes, and dances to his left. He tosses a few slow jabs at several people. The crowd, ever growing, erupts into laughter and applause. A space clears behind him and he uses it, knows it's there without turning to look. He walks backward, moving toward the far corner of the wide hallway, waving his audience forward, then turns to take his briefcase from me, pulling out a thick blue stack of Muslim tracts. Bingham reappears with a metal folding chair. Ali sits, places the briefcase on his lap, and produces an inexpensive pen from the pocket of his jacket.

Two minutes later, there's every bit of five hundred people in the hallway. A Mirage security guard uses his walkie-talkie to call for reinforcements and directs people who want autographs into a line.

I stand at Ali's right shoulder, against the wall. Bingham is to my left. We're in those positions for nearly an hour before I ask Bingham, "Is it always like this?"

"Always," he says. "Everywhere in the world. Last year, over two hundred thousand came to see him in Jakarta."

"How long will he do this?" I want to know, meaning today.

"Until he gets tired. For hours. All day."

Ali gives every person something personal. He talks to almost no one, yet most everyone seems to understand what he means. He gestures with his hands, fingers, head, eyes. He signs each person's first name on the Muslim literature and hugs and is hugged by everybody from three-year-old tykes to their eighty-year-plus great-grandmamas. Whenever kids are near, he goes out of his way to pick them up and snuggle and kiss them, sometimes more tenderly than one could imagine their own parents doing.

Women and men in line openly weep upon seeing Ali. Many recount stories about his impact on their lives. Some tell of having met him years before. He often pretends to remember. "You was wearin' a brown suit," he jokes with men. "You was in a blue dress," he tells women.

A huge, rough, Italian-looking man in his mid-forties takes Ali's hand, kisses it, then refuses an autograph. "I don't want anything from you, Champ," he says. His mud-brown eyes are red and swollen. "We've taken too much already."

I feel a need to touch Ali's shoulder. When I do, I'm sure he notices, but he doesn't react.

I stay with Ali a couple hours, but eventually have to leave to do a radio interview that my editor scheduled for me. Several times during the day, I pass Ali on the way to or from my room. Until late at night, he's signing and hugging and kissing and posing for photographs. There's always a line waiting for him that stretches around the corner and out of sight.

I have breakfast with Ali and Lonnie the next morning. He's wearing the same suit and tie. This isn't a sign of financial need or that he doesn't remember to change clothes. Even when he was fighting and earning tens of millions of dollars, he didn't own more than five suits. He seldom wears jewelry and his watch is a Timex.

I ask why, unlike the old days, everyone, everywhere, seems to love him. "Because I'm *baadd*," he clowns, then holds up his shaking left hand, spreads its fingers, and says, "It's because of this. I'm more human now. It's the God in people that connects them to me."

Twenty-three

I'm feeling significantly better by the time I get home from the Mirage, feeling the best I've felt since Daddy died. The only downside of the flight is a beginner's bout with jet lag, which keeps me swimmy-headed and in bed my first day back in Winston.

Lyn is at work and the kids are in school. When I'm finally able to roll out of bed, I've decided what I need to do to let Daddy go, what I can do to honor my father: I can go out and be as free as possible in this world it's not possible to be free in. That's what he'd want me to do: have as much life as the universe will allow.

I open every window in the house, finally put Metheny's *Letter from Home* on the stereo, take off all clothes except for a pair of red-and-white-striped boxers, and have myself a fine, purifying time, working out hard in the backyard, bathing my skin in the December sun. Who gives a fuck if anybody thinks I'm nuts?

"I have an idea for you," I tell my editor at *Sport*. "What about a piece called 'How to Beat Mike Tyson'?

"Everybody's talking this guy up," I continue, "making him sound indestructible. Just because he has a video game named after him doesn't mean he's superhuman. You wait and see—somebody's going to knock him off real soon."

"Okay," says my editor, "you've sold me. Let's do it. When's Tyson fighting next? We can run it just before his next fight."

Truth is, I don't give a rat's nose about Tyson per se. To me, he's not particularly interesting as a boxer or as a human being. Our world's heavyweight boxing champions have often mirrored the societies and years that spawned them. The one thing I'll give Tyson is this: As hardworking, elegantly stoic Joe Louis was exactly the right champ for the Depression years of the 1930s and war-effort forties, and ineffably bold, beautiful, and philosophic Ali was the ideal king for the expansive sixties and eclectic seventies, it's tough to imagine a more perfect world heavyweight than punk-chic, tree-trunk-thick Tyson for the "let's-grab-all-we-can" eighties, a decade when the abuse of extreme, even cartoonishly hypertrophic power was greatly admired by far too many people. Tyson, whose less-than-one-round knockouts are perfectly suited for the attention spans of MTV-trained juvies. But I can't accept Tyson being favorably compared to Ali the way he has been recently in the press as well as on the street, and I don't want him threatening my man's rep in any way. Besides, I know what it takes to whup "Kong," as Ali calls the current heavyweight champion. It's obvious.

"Much of what it will take to whip Tyson can be summarized simply," I write in my article. "It will take a tall, big fighter with a terrific chin, who has long arms and fast hands, who isn't afraid of Tyson, and who will be close to a complete boxer.

"He'll show Tyson many rhythms, keep him confused with different looks. It's crucial that he remain always poised—alert, yet relaxed—in all these styles. He need not be as beautiful in movement as Muhammad Ali, but it's likely he will have studied films of Ali's fights, and may have even idolized Ali."

The piece is published in the March issue of *Sport* magazine, available on newsstands two weeks before Tyson's February 10, 1990, bout. I send a copy of the piece to Ali, with a note that says he might be interested in what I've written. I let him know that the fantasy Tyson conqueror whose attributes I describe is, of course, none other than the Greatest of All Times.

On February 10, I'm asleep in bed when my office phone and the house line ring simultaneously a little before midnight.

Wondering what's wrong, I grope about the nightstand for the receiver. "He got knocked out!" Lyn's brother shouts in my ear. "They're counting over him right now!"

"Wh-what are you talking about?" I say, my mouth feeling like the pillow's still in it. "Who got knocked out?"

"Tyson! *Tyson* did!" says Scott. "He got knocked cold! He was down on the canvas fumbling around for his mouthpiece!"

I jump from bed as if something really important has happened. "Yes, yes, *yes!*" I shout into the receiver. "Lyn!" I yell, though she's lying right next to me. "Kong just got kayoed. Somebody knocked out Kong!"

"Who's 'Kong'?" my wife groggily asks.

"Scott, I'll call you tomorrow," I say. "I've got to go turn on the TV."

I buss Lyn on the cheek and fairly leap upstairs. The light is blinking on the answering machine, telling me I have a message. I turn off the ringer and the volume to the speaker and flip the TV to the sports channel. "Would you believe it?" a sculpted, white-bread announcer is saying. "In the first heavyweight championship fight of the 1990s, journeyman fighter James 'Buster' Douglas has knocked out the supposedly invincible Mike Tyson to become the new heavyweight champion of the world."

On screen, there are photos of Tyson's features getting reshaped by a long right hand, thrown Ali-style. Douglas looks to be about Ali's size; he's wearing Ali tassels on his shoes. And there's a shot of the new

champ mugging for the camera while being interviewed in the ring, mouth open and fist cocked beside his head in the Ali manner.

For a couple hours, I rove from channel to channel,
rejoicing in seeing Tyson get dumped flat on his
proper place in ring history, reveling in what this has
done for my career. I jump about the room throwing
jabs, stopping occasionally to whip out a combination
or explode into the shuffle. I feel twenty-two years
old. By the time I'm ready for bed, fourteen messages
have come in on the answering machine. The first
voice is my editor's. "Davis, this is Kelly. Congratulations. Give me a call first thing tomorrow."

The second message is also from someone I'm
pretty sure I recognize: "They gowna compare Tyson
to me now?" says the faceless caller, his unmistakable
voice sounding about as mighty as God's would be
echoing off of the moon.

By the time I get back with Kelly, *Sport* has received dozens of calls about my story. "We were getting them before the fight, too," he says, chuckling.
"Nearly everybody who wrote was critical of the idea
that Tyson could ever go down."

It's weird. On my answering machine I've got messages from newspapers all around the country, and
the Winston-Salem *Journal* is going to run a piece
about my Tyson article, as if I've actually accomplished something. I'm getting all this attention for

the closest thing to nonwriting I've done. How strange.

Kelly says he wants me to write profiles of Douglas and all the major heavyweight contenders, including old George Foreman, Evander Holyfield, and a follow-up Tyson piece. He'll publish an article every month for the next six months and will pay $2,000 per story. "I want you to be *Sport* magazine's boxing editor. You've earned it," he says. "I also want you to attend all major boxing events as our representative."

I ask if this means I'll be placed on payroll, if I'll have a salary."

"I wish it did," he says. "I can't even guarantee you a minimum amount of money each year. But I'll try to take care of you," he promises.

This'll bother Lyn some. She wants me to have a regular wage. But at least I can tell her that I'll make a minimum of twelve thousand from writing this year. And that, with her job and the interest from what's left of Daddy's inheritance, should be enough. I tell Kelly yes, I'll do it, not so much because I'm interested in boxing (I'm not), but because it'll give me greater opportunity to regularly spend time with Ali.

Twenty-four

Through Ali's influence, folks have become jazz musicians, dancers, basketballers, astronauts, environmentalists, stand-up comics, painters, chess champions, TV and movie producers and directors, rap singers, high-wire artists; they have joined the Peace Corps, become conscientious objectors, and yes, kickboxers and writers. Ray Leonard became "Sugar" Ray; Bruce Lee regularly studied film of Ali fights and emulated Ali's patterns of movement to become Bruce Lee, the god of movie martial art; Jimmy Connors was the first Ali of tennis (tennis brats—and every other sports punk since, including Mike Tyson—have unfortunately been in the Ali lineage); Nelson Mandela says he became Nelson Mandela partly because of Ali's influence.

James "Buster" Douglas is the most recent pugilist

to become heavyweight champion through Ali's stylistic influence. "He was my hero," Douglas tells me when I'm in Columbus to interview him for my piece. We're tooling around in his restored metallic-green 1970 Coupe de Ville. Douglas's window is down, mine is up, his left foot is out the window and on it is a size-fourteen blinding-red lizard-skin boot. Behind the footwear, he's sporting a grin about as big as Ohio Stadium. His round, smooth-skinned, good-hearted worker's face shines. It's the face Sonny Liston would have had, had he been a kind man. Douglas and I are chewing on oatmeal and raisin cookies he bought at a gas station.

"As an amateur, I tried to do everything I saw Ali do," says Douglas. "Used to wear trunks like his, white with black stripes, still wear Ali tassels. Only *arteests* wear tassels. I learned a lot from Ali. Learned to be nice to people. Got to meet him in Huntington, West Virginia, last week. He went to dinner with me, told me how happy it made him that I won. He jumped two feet out of his chair with his hands over his head and said that's what he did when I knocked out Short Man."

I ask Douglas to sign a copy of my Tyson piece. "Man, I read this on the plane to Tokyo for the fight. Everybody in my corner was passin' this around the plane."

He takes a pen from my hand. MIKE TYSON CAN BE BEAT, reads the headline. Above the title, in bold blue letters, Douglas writes, "And I'm The Man That Done It."

Twenty-five

Ali's father dies of heart disease. When I hear the news, I call the Clay residence to give my condolences.

Lonnie answers the phone.

"How's he taking it?" I ask.

"Better than I thought he would," she answers.

I ask to speak with Mrs. Clay, who tells me, "Even fifty years ago, my husband always said he'd die at seventy-seven. I guess he was right. He lived a full life."

I don't talk to the Champ. I ask Mrs. Clay to say hello for me.

Twenty-six

In Miami International Airport, I unexpectedly run into Ali on my way to spend a couple days with George Foreman in Houston. As usual, Ali's at the center of a crowd and people are looking at him with the same sweet sadness they ordinarily reserve for a favorite uncle who has recently suffered a stroke.

He's not surprised to see me. He's wearing black and carrying about a hundred of his Muslim handouts. His face is puffy; he looks exhausted.

"Been to see Angelo Dundee," he tells me. "Tired of travelin'. Before this, I was in Saudi Arabia. It's too Western—a holy place they've made so American. They care too much about money and possessions."

I ask if he'd like a root beer. We walk a couple hundred yards to a coffee shop. A few people follow along until we go inside.

As we enter, he spots a woman with her head folded into her arms, slumped across a table. He takes a seat beside her and asks what's wrong. She looks up and doesn't seem to recognize Ali, but tells him her purse has been stolen. The woman is short and dumpy, and she's wearing a pink warm-up suit. She has graying black hair and deep-set green eyes that bulge as if someone has grabbed her around the neck and squeezed, not real hard, but steadily, for many, many years.

She laughs wearily. "It had all my money in it. I don't know how I'm going to get home. And how can I tell my husband? He don't like me spendin' so much, anyways. It's got me all *flustrated* sometimes. Sometimes we have some real blowouts over money."

Ali puts his pamphlets on the table and pulls a tattered brown cowhide wallet from his pants pocket. It has $300 cash in it and an old picture of him with all eight of his kids. He gives the woman $280.

We never get our root beers. Soon he's out in the airport again. I watch him with children, making faces, trading punches, tickling, hugging, kissing.

I ask why he connects so to children.

"I'm a big kid myself," he says. And: "They're angels in exile," he replies, speaking in the same tone you'd expect from a monk exposing the uninitiated to the mysteries. "Children are so close to God. They haven't had time to separate from Him."

Twenty-seven

A four-inch-long lizard the color of southeast Texas dust scurries about the surface of a big, free-standing white sign with hand-painted olive lettering. The lizard is looking for a place to hide and it can't find one. It jumps nervously to the ground and scratches away into thin brown grass around a cluster of scraggly pines. The sign from which the lizard has leapt reads CHURCH OF THE LORD JESUS CHRIST.

It's Sunday, almost ten A.M. The Reverend George Edward Foreman is standing under an overhang beside the beige corrugated metal building that functions as his sanctuary. Foreman looks as if he might have appeared out of the very ground around the church. Sweat runs in beaded rivulets down his forehead and the sides of his face. He's wearing a black vest that's too tight to button, a pair of almost matching trousers, and a thin, inexpensive short-sleeve white shirt that can hardly contain his arms and neck. The fabric is stretched almost to the ripping point. His right foot is propped on the second stair of the concrete steps that lead into the church. He welcomes his fold as they enter.

Inside, on a small platform, a long-faced, thick-shouldered man in his thirties sits on a stool and strums a shining Gibson guitar while singing a happy-sounding hymn. Compared to the stark exterior, the comfort and attractiveness of the small room is surprising. The walls are the color of lime sherbet, and two large arrangements of tiger lilies and orchids adorn opposite sides of the pulpit. There are six rows of well-maintained dark oak pews, enough seating for maybe seventy-five people. Not a third that many are in attendance today.

Throughout his sermon, Pastor Foreman howls and prowls, back and forth, up and down, his tone sounding like a stand-up comedian's imitation of Ali. He warns not to take that drink on Saturday night and not to lay with that inviting stranger. "Some people don't even believe in a supernatural God," he shouts near the end of his message. "I wouldn't serve a god who wouldn't speak to me. I was talkin' to a fella one time and he told me he turned toward somewhere and prayed eight or nine times a day. And he showed me how he put his head down to the ground. I said, 'Man, does God ever speak to you?' He said, 'No.' I said, 'Hey, brother, ain't nobody home.'"

On the way out the door at the end of the sermon, I ask Foreman to confirm that his story was about Ali.

"That's him," he says. "I know the hand of God is on him. He's being told, 'Hey, you been callin' the wrong man.' Most of his greatest gifts been taken away, like puttin' a microscope on a fly and a pair of tweezers. Take a wing, take a leg, take this, take that, until there's nothin' left. God only takes a man up for one reason: to cut him down. That's why I try to stay in the basement."

Twenty-eight

Midafternoon, July 17, 1990. Johanna's ninth birthday. I'm in my study working on the Foreman piece, trying to wrap it up as quick as possible. Tonight there'll be cake and ice cream, rented movies, and a sleepover for Johanna's friends. I glance at Daddy's watch, wondering when Lyn and the kids'll get home from work and day care, then I look again. It reads 11:17. Well, how about that? The second hand has stopped. The battery must've gone dead; Daddy's timepiece has quit. I carefully remove the watch from my arm and place it on the left corner of the desk, beside his Social Security card. The imprint in my flesh will disappear within an hour. When the universe tells you something this directly, you've just got to listen.

*   *   *

August 1990. Like last summer, it's happening again. The air is dense with heat. Good ole global warming.

In so many ways, life is getting better for most of us. It seems more and more miraculous, there are greater and greater possibilities, all the time. If we can manage to survive the lower atmosphere ozone buildup, upper atmosphere ozone depletion, the daily, weekly, monthly, yearly killing off of forests, oceans, waterways (and every other fucking thing), the dramatic overcrowding of the planet, if we can somehow manage to reduce the world's population by a couple billion to a number the groaning planet can comfortably sustain, maybe it'll keep on getting better still. What a remarkable time to be alive.

Today, it's over one hundred degrees. None of the horses on the farms along I-64 between Lexington and Louisville are out in the sun; I suppose they're sipping chilled water in their multimillion-dollar CFC air-conditioned barns. I'm passing through Kentucky on the way to Detroit for an interview with Thomas Hearns.

Ali greets me at the door to his mom's house. He's wearing a sky-blue seersucker safari suit and the same pair of white sneakers he had on the first day I met him. His face has lost much of its puffiness. In this moment, he looks like the Ali of the seventies. "My man," he says.

Ali still doesn't know my name. I'm convinced this isn't indicative of serious mind-fry. It's more a function of having met probably half the people on the planet. Most important, though, it's related to a choice he made long ago not to burden his spirit with meaningless surface details.

"You look good," I tell him. "How much weight you lost?"

"Can you really tell?" he asks, sounding flattered. "I'm down to two-twenty-four." That's the least he's weighed since 1980. In the final years of his career, he fought in the mid-220s. "Goin' all the way to two-ten. Won't eat nothin' but chicken and fish, fruit and vegetables. No grease. Drink lots of water." His voice seems different, a bit stronger. There's no longer a wet sound in his throat when he speaks.

"You're starting to look pretty again. Are you working out?"

"I'm trainin'. Started by walkin' twenty-five miles a day. I'm not walkin' no more. Doin' five rounds heavy bag, five speed bag, five shadowboxin'."

I step into the foyer. "I'm trainin' for a spiritual battle," he says as he closes the door behind me.

It is four weeks since Iraq invaded Kuwait. Soldiers of Western nations are massing at the Saudi Arabian border. This morning on NPR a commentator said that there may soon be a half million American troops in the area.

I follow Ali to the kitchen. He pulls a quart bottle of mineral water from the refrigerator and downs about a third of it in one bubbling gulp. I take a chair at a cream-colored, chrome-trimmed dinette table. Cassius Clay, Sr.'s stained and yellowed registration card for a 1972 Cadillac is propped between the salt and pepper shakers. The room is hot and musty. I pick up the piece of paper and think about Daddy's Social Security card and watch on my desk at home. "How do you feel?" I ask.

"Got more energy. Move better."

Mrs. Clay comes into the room. "Oh, I'm so glad you're here," she says to me. She's wearing a yellow paisley dress and smells of flour. Although she seems tired and a light sweat shines on her forehead and neck, she smiles her fragile smile. "Would you like a glass of root beer?"

She brings the soda in an old Welch's jelly glass. Ali leaves the room to say his midday prayers.

"Doesn't he look better?" she says, sounding hopeful. "I told you he did. He looks so young. It makes him feel like he can fight again. He couldn't do that, could he?"

"No," I say. "No one would let him."

She looks relieved. "Before the Foreman fight," she says, "everybody was so nervous, thought he'd lose, maybe even get hurt. He told me he'd win, but he was the only one who was sure. In the corner, when he was praying, I saw bright lights all around him and knew he would win. Now he doesn't talk anymore. He's so quiet you forget he's in the house. He reads and writes, writes and reads all the time."

Ali returns to the kitchen, still barefoot from his prayers, moving so quietly I can't help but believe he's trying not to disturb even the dust beneath his feet. In this outfit, he looks like an Indian holy man. He waves for me to follow him. We go downstairs and sit side by side on the sofa. As usual, he flips on the television. A popular M.C. Hammer video is playing. He studies the bodies jumping across the screen and says, "Looks foolish. What do you think?"

I think so, too.

"Black folks always foolin' themselves," he comments. "Need somebody so bad, they turn anybody into a hero. Pimps, pushers, it don't matter who."

A gold-framed certificate I haven't seen before is hanging crooked above the TV. I get up to see what's on it.

"In Memoriam," it reads, "the Los Angeles County Board of Supervisors extends its deepest sympathy to you in the passing of your beloved father, Cassius Marcellus Clay, in whose memory all members adjourned in tribute and reverence at its meeting of February 13, 1990."

I straighten the plaque.

"It was a relief," Ali says before I have a chance to ask. "He was gettin' so old, in so much pain all the time. Talked to him a week before he died. He said he wouldn't see me again. 'I'm tired,' he said. 'Tired of this pacemaker. Don't want it no more.' It happens to all of us. It'll happen to me before long, it'll happen to you. We all get tired. We'll close our eyes and won't open them again. I'm preparin' myself for the next life. That's what matters now."

The phone rings. He answers. "They'll be killin' each other," he says into the receiver. "Don't want that to happen."

He's on the phone about fifteen minutes—a long time for Ali. He talks some, but mostly listens. The male voice on the other end is loud and deep.

When Ali hangs up, he tells me, "I'm glad you're here. I need some advice." The look on his face is serious.

"People want me to go to Iraq and Saudi Arabia," he explains. "Stand between two big armies gettin' ready to fight. They want me to put up my arms and say, 'I'm Muhammad Ali. Don't shoot.' They believe I can stop the war. Do you think I should do it?"

"Well . . . I don't know. It's not something I'd do." I want to be gentle, but would also like to discourage him.

He appears to drop the subject, and leaves the room. Mrs. Clay brings lunch. Tuna sandwiches on white bread, canned peaches and pears. Ali returns with a portable cassette player I'd given him the last time I saw him. He's playing a sermon. He has dozens of Muslim lectures and messages, but until I offered him the recorder I'd been using to tape interviews, he had nothing on which to play them when he was traveling. The speaker's voice sounds a little warbled. The batteries are losing power; I'm sure he won't replace them when they go dead. We eat slowly, without talking, as Ali listens to the sermon. When he's through eating, he pushes the stop button and looks at me.

"Why have you followed me so long?" he asks, looking genuinely puzzled. I feel the full weight of him as he watches me.

"It's because you're the single largest person I've ever known," I say, meaning not so much his physical size, thinking about how Ali has always harbored opposing ideas and that in some very real way, it has almost nothing to do with the things he's seen, the life he's lived, the privileges he's known. It's bigger, rounder, more elemental. We connect with Ali not only for what he has done, but simply for who he is. (It was he who got me interested in fighting, not the fighting that got me interested in him.) If Cassius Marcellus Clay, Jr., had never laced a pair of shining leather mitts, something would have happened to make him one of the most influential people of this century, to have created a mythology that would be finally hopeful, wonderful, sad, beautiful.

He nods. "I've traveled the whole world," he says. "Learn somethin' from people everywhere. Watch children and see myself not long ago. See old folks and know it's even less time before I'm one of them. Then I think, 'I already *am* one of them.' There ain't no differences between us. There's truth in Hinduism, Christianity, Islam, all religions. And in just plain talkin'. The only religion that matters is the real religion—love."

As I listen to Ali, a cosmic *yes!* roars up from my belly. We seek connection, not recognizing that there is nothing we need do to become: the shape of tree trunks and of branches, the form of our limbs and torsos, the rhythms I feel rotating inside me; the shape of hurricanes and of galaxies, the orbits of planets and of neutrons—so very similar. Everything is at the center: rocks, pig excrement, penises, Popsicles, pumpkins, breasts; electrons, stars, these cold fingers, us, everything: the gold we wear around our fingers and necks, the calcium that makes up our bones—both from the marrow of long-ago-exploded stars. We are, each of us, even in the strictest, most literal sense, the very stuff of the cosmos.

Ali and I return to the sofa. I ask about his prayers; he shows me a book that details the way for Muslims to pray.

He says, "I'm tired. I need a nap. The heat's botherin' me." The words sound ancient, totemic. "Are you gowna be here when I wake up?" he asks.

"I think I better go. I have work to do."

He reaches to hug me, all the while watching my eyes. His body is so thick, his skin cool and moist through the thin shirt. I remember rubbing Daddy's back and shoulders in the hospital. Next Tuesday, it'll be exactly one year since he died. Ali smells of earth and of trees. I kiss him on the cheek.

"Be cool and look out for the ladies," he says.

In November, Ali travels to Baghdad to make a plea for peace. At the end of his ten-day mission, he returns to New York with fifteen Americans who had been held hostage for over four months.

Twenty-nine

Although the magazine doesn't pay well, Kelly does a pretty good job of picking up travel expenses (or at least promising to pick them up; it sometimes takes six months to get reimbursed for charges on my MasterCard and Visa). One thing that seems unfair, however, is that over a two-year period I'm asked to attend more than fifty fights and numerous events as the magazine's representative. But I receive no pay for the travel or for the radio and TV interviews. Kelly says that the owner does it this way so he won't have to hire PR people.

In April, I'm in Philadelphia for a dinner marking the twentieth anniversary of the first Frazier fight. This morning, Ali has been at Frazier's gym, signing autographs for children. He quit training during his stay in Iraq and has gained a lot of weight. He's at probably 250, but as always, he is standing erect against the burden of gravity.

As we leave the gym, I slide into the limo and take a seat across from the Champ. An elderly man who looks a little like Ali's dead father startlingly appears beside the limousine. He taps on my window with his left knuckles. I jump. "Mr. Clay, Mr. Clay," he shouts, and offers Ali (who never eats pork) a hot dog. He's razor-thin and his eyes are yellow with age, cheap wine, and a life spent on street corners.

Ali motions me to lower my window. He takes the old guy's hand for a moment.

As we leave the curb, I ask, "Do you let everybody in?" I've never seen him refuse anyone.

"I'm glad people care about me. It's a blessin'. Don't want to disappoint nobody. But there's a lot of people who hurt you without meanin' to."

As I've told you before, it's not that there's anything particularly special about my relationship with Ali, except that it's mine (and that I can write about him in a way no one else has). He treats almost everyone exactly the way he treats me. This is part of the miracle of Ali. It's hard to imagine that there has ever been anyone else quite like him, and it's doubtful there ever will be again.

We pull up to a stoplight. To my left, a heavy woman, dressed in browns and grays, who has no legs or hands, is propped against a doorway. She's playing "Amazing Grace" on a harmonica that has been attached to her mouth by a strand of what looks to be plastic clothesline. "We don't know how that lady got

here," says Ali. "She's just like you and me." His left
hand begins to dramatically tremble. We near the
Hotel Atop the Bellevue, where we're staying. Ali
closes his eyes and drops into a light sleep.

In this moment, regardless of what he said in the
sixties, it's obvious that this man has not made himself Muhammad Ali; it's not a life or role of his own
choosing. Sometimes it appears that his own life
doesn't even matter to him. It's now part of Ali's mul-
tiplicitousness to think of his life as no more important than anyone else's. Who is this man, really? I
study the shape of his head, watch its almost perfect
symmetry, his skin's baby smoothness. He looks like a
sleeping newborn, or a Buddha. Surely his is an ancient soul. Perhaps he's some kind of bodhisattva.
And maybe he's also a little like Chance, the gar-
dener, in Jerzy Kosinski's novel *Being There*—a slate
onto which we write what we wish, a screen onto
which most anything can be projected—mysteries
swirling through his life which *appear* to have meaning but which no one quite understands.

As we step from the limo in front of the hotel,
there's a crowd of several hundred on the sidewalk
and spilling over into the street.

Near the outside of this group, an Asian man in his
thirties places his young son on his shoulders, where
he can get a clean look at the Champ. "That's the
greatest man in the world," he says to his boy in a
rolling Southern accent. When he's able to make it to
Ali, the man asks for an autograph for his son and

tells Ali that he came to see him all the way from his home in Arkansas. I walk along the fringe of this troop, then enter the hotel.

The Ali family is congregating in the lobby. There's Bingham and Ali's daughters Miya and May May, a rap singer who looks a little like Janet Jackson. Mrs. Clay is sitting in a high wingback chair. "Oh, I didn't know you'd be here," she says. "I'm so happy to see you." She's lost a few pounds and looks even more frail than usual. She's recently suffered a stroke and isn't recovering well.

Lonnie is standing beside Mrs. Clay. She has an oversized blue canvas bag slung over her right shoulder and a quite young infant in her arms.

"Hi, Lonnie," I say. "Whose baby?"

"He's ours," she says, and laughs because I'm stunned by this news; my mouth is hanging open. "Doesn't he look like Muhammad?"

She lowers the baby where I can have a peek. The child's countenance and complexion are flawless, like her husband's, and the baby's skin is an identical glowing copper color.

"He does look like Muhammad," I say. "What's his name?"

"Ask Muhammad," she says, frowning. "He says he's going to name the baby, but you know Muhammad—he can't make up his mind. He wants to call him Ahad, which means 'the one and only.' I keep telling him that's not the right name for a Muslim baby."

"How old is he?"

"He'll be one month tomorrow," she answers.

I step back and take a peek at her body. Her face is maybe a little drawn but she doesn't look like she's had a child within the past four weeks.

"We're adopting him," she explains. "We're waiting for the papers to come from Louisville."

As Ali makes it to the lobby, he reaches for his new son, pulling the baby to his face and kissing and holding it to his right cheek with almost unbearable tenderness. In this moment, Ali looks as pleased as anyone I've ever seen.

"Didn't get to see the other eight growin' up," the proud papa says with profundity. "I'm gowna enjoy this baby."

"It's good to have something new in your life," I say, "something that's growing."

"Want to have five more," he tells me. "All races. When I'm seventy-five years old, they'll be twenty."

"Are you serious?" I ask, although this melds into his mythology—Muhammad Ali the international man, Ali the champion granddaddy of the whole wide world.

"Naw, it's just a dream," he says. "I know it's a dream."

"Sometimes it's good to dream," I tell him. "'The man without imagination has no wings; he cannot fly,'" I say, quoting a favorite Ali phrase from the seventies.

We're sitting at a dining table in the Ali suite. Ali is trying to feed his son from a bottle while Lonnie orders room service. He pours milk all over the baby's face. The boy's head is at the wrong angle and, despite having fathered eight kids by four mothers, the old fighter isn't experienced enough at the feeding ritual to recognize he's doing this all wrong.

Lonnie hurries from across the room. "Muhammad, let me have that child before you drown him," she scolds.

While waiting on lunch, Lonnie suggests a name—Asaad Amin Ali. "It means son of the lion," she says. It would be tough to imagine a more perfect moniker.

Her husband nods his approval.

Throughout the day, a near-constant processional flows in and out of the Ali suite. Philadelphia-area Muslims offer vegetarian dinners and sweet bean pies; a fellow who makes Muhammad Ali chocolate chip cookies and potato chips brings samples, of which Ali himself munches bag after bag; Ali intimates I recognize from TV screens joke and kid and hug the Champ. Baby Asaad is regularly brought out of the bedroom and is shown all around. Ali is chuckling and smiling and sneaking up behind people making cricket noises with his fingers. Rahaman gets in from Louisville. He, Bingham, and Ali shove and wrestle around the room while Mrs. Clay watches. Ali backs Bingham into a corner with goofy, looping punches. Bingham kicks toward Ali's groin to make him back off. "He knows better than to mess with me," says Ali's best friend. "I ain't afraid of him. He knows it'll cost him."

"Just like the old days," Mrs. Clay says to me. "Nothing's changed a bit."

Rahaman tells Lonnie that he doesn't have a place to stay and that the hotel is sold out. I offer to let him room with me. For whatever reason, Rock finds this idea hilarious. He laughs and hisses and bends over and covers his face with his hands. But he takes me up on my offer.

Over fifteen hundred patrons have paid $250 per plate for the privilege of eating dinner in the same room with Ali and Frazier. In the big anteroom, a much larger tide, maybe three thousand folks, lap up against the Ali island as we make our way toward the ballroom. As Ali enters the room, the old primal chant goes up: *"Ahh-lee! Ahh-lee! Ahh-lee!"*

Before he allows himself to be seated, he walks over to Frazier and attempts to kiss his old foe on the cheek. Frazier leans away from Ali's attentions and glares a hard man's glare.

Ali's chair is on the right side of the dais, Frazier's is on the left. Sitting behind the white cloth-covered table, with candlelight playing across his face, Ali drops in and out of sleep.

Frazier gets up to make a speech. "Twenty years later, he's still tryin' to start somethin'," he says, glowering. "He got himself in trouble to begin with because he wouldn't let me say nothin'. Now, when I'm talkin', he comes up behind me, makin' a noise like he's stickin' a bug or somethin' in my ear. He can't even talk no more, but he's always tryin' to make noise. Always messin' with me."

Frazier chooses not to get over having been called an Uncle Tom and a gorilla and generally having been treated as an inferior by a less mature Ali. Publicly *and* among his intimates, Ali says that he loves Joe Frazier, that he's sorry he hurt him, and that he wishes Joe would forgive him.

May May steps up to the platform and drapes her arms about her dad. She whispers in his ear. He turns and smiles that easiest of smiles for her, the one we all remember. And then he laughs. He's having a good time.

Moments later, she returns to her seat at the Ali family table, which is right beside mine. I look at Lonnie and the baby, Miya and May May, Mrs. Clay and Rahaman, and wonder, with Mrs. Clay's health being as tenuous as it is, if this group will appear together in public again.

Ali picks up a piece of bread and begins to eat. He's the only person on the dais who's doing so, but he's not self-conscious. Through the speakers' introductions and the opening invocation by a Christian minister, he continues to chomp away. When he finishes the bread, he gets up from his seat, reaches behind the podium, and pulls a stack of tracts from his briefcase, which he begins to sign. He stops only when the lights have been dimmed and Frazier's son Marvis tells us that we'll be viewing highlights from the 1971 fight between his dad and Ali. On the screen, Ali is wearing red velvet trunks, Frazier's are an iridescent green—exact opposites on the color wheel—and you can still feel the heat between these two come shimmering off of the screen.

I glance from the twenty-year-old film to the now-silent man who's sitting in candlelight not six feet from me. He has covered his eyes with his right hand. He is asleep and snoring.

Thirty

I travel more and more regularly to boxing events, sometimes enjoying the bouts, but not the travel. The magazine won't pay Lyn's expenses to accompany me, and we can't afford to do so ourselves, so I'm always alone on the road. And by mid-1991, Ali has almost stopped making appearances at big boxing shows.

One thing I get a kick out of in press rooms before fights is hearing reporters who were around in the sixties and seventies tell their Ali stories. These grizzled and groaning old coots invariably lament Ali's health. The intimation: "You youngsters shoulda been around then, when he was really Ali." Like the rest of us, they expect Our Black Dorian Gray to have remained a glowing young athlete through perpetuity. It doesn't take a lot to recognize that the problem here is not so much with Ali, and his malady, as it is with the reporters themselves. These guys, almost none of whom have access to the current Ali, feel the subconscious need to protect their memories of him (translation: their own personal territory—indeed, *their lives*). In effect, it is for themselves that they mourn more than it is for Ali—as it is myself that I'm protecting and mourning when I call these fellows "grizzled and groaning old coots."

After hanging out at maybe a hundred fights and writing a few heavyweight profiles and a couple other pieces that earn more and more respect for my work (Kelly and I agree that the quality of our boxing coverage now rivals that of *Sports Illustrated*, for which I'm not allowed to write, since *S.I.* is a direct competitor), and getting fewer and fewer assignments from *Sport* (the owner and the publisher both tell Kelly that boxing doesn't merit all these pieces, and when looked at as a way to sell magazines, they're right), I realize that Daddy's money is trickling away. Although my pieces are regularly quoted on TV and in numerous big-city newspapers, no matter how many hours I put in, how good my stories are, and how much media attention they receive, I'm still unable to make a living.

I read the results of a survey for which folks were asked what they'd be doing if they could pick a job, any job. The number-one choice was to be a writer, to write for a living. The reality is this: Professional writing is even more competitive than pro sports. Less than two hundred people in this country are able to make a living at what I'm trying to do: sell stories freelance to magazines and newspapers. Yet I remain certain that everything will work out. As Ali was born to box, I'm in this world to write.

Although I don't much respect or enjoy journalism, I'm pretty good at it, in my own way. I don't separate myself from people I interview. Indeed, I try not to write *about* people at all, but *with* them. People I talk with almost always let me know they're telling me stuff they've never told anyone. Vying for access, reporters and photographers are visibly surprised by the time I'm given, at the intimacy I develop with folks I write about. I'm pretty sure I know why this happens, why I get this close to people: Fighters are uncommonly instinctive. They understand that I won't hurt them. More important (and as hokey as it sounds), I believe that they sense the connectedness, that I, like them, have had the shit kicked out of me, and that I respect them and understand what they do.

Over a couple years, I get tight not only with Ali, but with Leonard, Douglas, Foreman, Pernell Whitaker, and with Hector "Macho" Camacho, who tells me that in a stadium before a Julio Cesar Chavez fight (Camacho's arch foe), he was cornered by a pack of Chavez fans. "I was in trouble, man. They was gonna cut me up."

Just when he saw no place to turn, Ali stepped out of a tunnel on the way to his seat. "Man, he saved me. Ali saved me. He came over and did that funny little wave he does with his hand cupped behind his back, showing me to follow him. I tucked in behind, just like he was my mama, and he took me down ringside."

By mid-1991, other than what I've put away for college for the kids and the equity in our house, Daddy's money has been spent and is gone. When I'm not traveling for *Sport*, I start taking quickie assignments (the equivalent of fighting three-round smokers in honky-tonks) for all sorts of publications. "We need this in five days," editors tell me. "We'll pay two hundred dollars. Throw something together."

My work pattern goes like this: After maybe a one-hour phone interview, I pace around the house for two to three days, being seriously irritable, before I finally get ideas. I write a graph or two, which I may or may not use, then read a few pages of Louise Erdrich, Tim O'Brien, Joan Didion, Richard Ford, John Irving, drop-your-jaw extraordinary work, not at all like the tricks I have to turn to try to eke out a living. I walk through the neighborhood, watch wind, trees, sky, then lock myself in my office. After three to four hours of intense sitting, the first usable paragraph typically arrives. By this time, I'm spent. I take a half-hour nap to empty the mind, then write again and again; smearing peanut butter on bread and calling it a meal, making three to five phone calls hoping to wrangle more work, writing two more hours or until I simply can't do it anymore, napping again, taking Dallas for a walk around the block or throwing his Frisbee to him in the backyard, doing a few push-ups or crunches or leg raises, still more napping, three to five rounds on the bag, another hour or two at the keyboard; waiting, wishing, aching for the kids to go to bed so I can think more crisply, then in the sack myself by nine at the latest; up at two A.M. to start over again; working for three hours, then back to bed until eight; following this general pattern until the piece is complete, which is usually late on the day of the deadline. I sneak one real paragraph or sentence or phrase into every article, at least one moment of the genuine stuff, something to which I'll be proud to attach my name.

"We have to have the piece right now," I'm told on the deadline date or before, so I fax it in or modem it or Fed Ex it, then wait at least two weeks, despite making phone calls almost daily, before the editor, any editor, every editor, reads it, and a minimum of another ten days before he/she decides whether she/he likes it, then an average of two months before a check is cut, if the article is accepted—which, almost as often as not, it isn't.

Around this same time, an editor I regularly work with goes schizo on cocaine. Before he's fired he costs me more than $12,000 in assignments he forgot he had made and expenses to and from places he didn't remember he had sent me. Although the magazine's publisher says that he'll make it up to me, I never manage to recover the lost revenue.

Doesn't sound much like what you thought, does it? Ain't exactly the high life, huh?

Then, there are the *other stories,* the ones that always fuel me, that are my beautiful, gleaming children of smoke and bones, spit and dreams.

6 May, 1991

Mr. Michael Caruso, Senior Editor
Vanity Fair
350 Madison Avenue
New York, NY 10017

Dear Michael Caruso:

   Enjoyed speaking with you yesterday. As I mentioned on the phone, I have a story that I believe will interest you. I'd like to write a 5,000 to 7,000 word piece that I would call, "The Zen of Muhammad Ali." Access to the reclusive Ali is not a problem: I met him several years ago and ever since, have regularly spent time with him and have talked with him on the phone.

   This access has allowed me to see much that is not widely recognized by the media, including not only that Ali's health is considerably different from what has been reported, but that his worldwide popularity has hardly diminished since his retirement from boxing. Ali travels nearly 300 days of each year; throngs turn out to greet him wherever he goes.

   In the years since the onset of Ali's Parkinson's syndrome, he has become intensely dedicated to a pursuit of the spiritual. "The Zen of Muhammad Ali" will propose a new Ali mythology, part of which is related to the idea of Ali as mystic, or, more precisely, as a vessel into which enlightenment pours, and from which it flows, sometimes in ways that Ali himself doesn't recognize. On a recent visit to his mother's house in Louisville, Ali told me, "God's usin' me."

Intrigued, I asked him, "What's he using you for?"

"I don't know," he said. "And it don't matter if I know. What matters is He's doing it, He's always done it."

In March of this year, over a quarter of a million people came to see Ali in Jerusalem. It's in no way an overstatement to say that Ali has tens of millions of fans. The basic reason that we don't see much about him in the press is that he doesn't want to be written about: A seeming paradox about Ali is that, although he is accessible to almost everyone on the street, everywhere, he feels that media coverage would violate the spiritual nature of his life.

In many ways, Ali exemplifies that which is classically Buddhist. Although there is a fragility about him, there is also that which seems eternal. He regularly sits on the edge of conversations, listening. The art of the gesture has become quite important for Ali. He communicates with his hands, his head, his eyes. He surprises visitors by making a sound with his fingers that's not unlike a cricket in your ear, he blows on the top of heads, tickles the inside of palms as he shakes hands, does assorted prestidigitations: "Wake up, wake up," call these nontraditional koans. These qualities are (part of) the Zen of Muhammad Ali.

It goes without saying that Ali is not just another retired athlete: He is the most recognizable person of the 20th century. People all over the globe admire Ali not only for the obvious reasons: the singular grace with which he fought for almost twenty-five years, his boastful prettiness, his huge charm and presence, his contagious and distinct humor, his brave stand against the Vietnam War (and all war), but also for the great dignity with which he has carried himself through his afflicted middle years. Indeed, a positive thing about Ali's Parkinson's syndrome is that it has helped him become everybody's grandfather; his malady has given us all the opportunity to continue to care about him.

I think that my story will have nearly timeless and universal appeal. I'm not uncomfortable saying that it will be quite unlike anything that has ever been written about the world's most famous man. I look forward to soon hearing back from you and hopefully to working with you on this piece.

All best,
Davis Miller

Despite similar letters and phone calls to a cornucopia of magazine editors, I have bigtime difficulty finding a buyer for "Zen." Over the phone, I swear I hear one editor wince as he says, "Ali is entirely too painful to read about." It does no good to tell the editor (again) that Ali's story is not tragic.

Lots of hardcore New York editors say that what I want to do isn't dark or sensational enough. A number of them say that there's no market among their readers for a new Ali piece. But this story is important, I *have* to tell it, and I believe that I'll eventually find an editor somewhere who shares some of my values and sensibilities. And I'm right: after almost a year of looking, there he is. And he's the guy in charge at a big, new, men's monthly that's planning its first issue. He offers me the best money I've ever been paid—$8,500. Before taking this job, he was at *Outside* magazine. He has a tender voice and he's a good listener. And I'm sure that I'll have a fine time working with him.

He asks me to hook up with Ali as soon as possible and to try to get the piece in within a couple months. A real bonus is that he offers to pay one-half of the fee in advance and agrees to $5,000 in expenses for me to go hang with the Champ.

Hell, if I had the money, I'd pay the editor for the privilege.

It's shortly after dawn. A pudding-thick fog shines through the South Carolina peat bog as the gray stretch Lincoln limousine glides up U.S. Highway 17 from Charleston airport to Myrtle Beach.

Ali is sitting directly across from me on the seat closest to the rear of the car. There are two ballpoint pens in his shirt pocket and many streaks of blue ink mar the fabric near the pens.

"Just got back from China," he says. "When I left, five hundred thousand people followed me to the airport. Been travelin' too much. I'm tired. All the stuff people make, all the things we think's important, a big wind could come up and blow it all away."

A documentary about Hugo is being played on the limo's VCR. We pass an ancient pine forest that the driver says had been so thick before Hugo that you couldn't see twenty feet into it. The Atlantic can now be spotted about a half mile to the east.

As I'm looking out the window, Ali falls to sleep and begins to snore. He sits slumped with his hands in his lap. I notice for the first time how much his hairline has receded. It has been a few weeks since he's had his hair colored and it has gone white at the temples. As usual, the fingers of his left hand begin to twitch. But something's different. These are not his typical tremors. As he continues to snore, the movement becomes recognizable: He's throwing short, spasmodic punches—first the jab, about once every ten seconds, and after thirty seconds or so, he drops the straight right. Just when I begin to wonder if his health is worse than I've thought, he squints open his right eye and winks at me. When he's sure I've gotten his joke, he opens both eyes, sits up, and chuckles.

"Fooled you, didn't I?" he says. The old trickster is at it again, exploiting the punch-drunk rumors, the concern we all have for his health. I'm reminded of one of his favorite tactics in the latter years of his career—of making his legs wobble when he'd been caught with good shots—of pretending to be hurt worse than he was. But, certainly, as the Ali of the seventies was stunned when he feigned being on the verge of getting knocked into the Great Abyss, the nineties version had fallen into a light sleep and had roused himself (and made me feel better) with his own joke.

*   *   *

Ali says he's gotten little rest on the plane from China, yet two hours after he checks into a hotel, he's scheduled to make an appearance at a car dealership.

In the limo, he keeps his tinted window down so that passersby will see him. As always, when he's recognized, people wave, cheer, yell. At the dealership, a crowd of hundreds is waiting. The owner of the dealership escorts Ali to a metal table and folding chair. He pulls one of the ballpoints from his pocket and prepares to write.

I sit beside him and hand him tracts one by one. He signs until he gives out all of them, then autographs scraps of paper, dollar bills, copies of old books and magazines, pictures of children, at least one Koran, two Bibles, and a Vietnam prisoner of war's photograph of himself. He whispers in my ear: "I've signed my name more than anybody in the history of the world."

This driven, crazed, marvelously insane man. Simply watching him work for hour upon hour exhausts me. So many lives! Expecting, wanting, hoping to be lifted from the dust, if only for a moment.

How is my own, personal insanity any different?

I've learned from Ali not to fight the insanity, but to accept it. My need to feel immortal, to be connected—there's a beauty to it. As there is to the mad(e)ness, the manic creative synergy, within many of us.

A roundish woman in a flowered dress appears to my left and says, "Please make it to Chuck, my husband. He's afraid to ask for himself." She turns and points. A fellow about my age but looking much older, with a farmer's sun-damaged face and a red, scraggly beard and swollen eyes, is leaning against the wall, hiding in the far corner. Ali tries to return the open ink pen to his shirt pocket and misses, staining his shirt with another blue stripe. He motions the man forward and takes his hand.

"I want you to know you're my hero," the man says, still hanging back behind his wife, obviously embarrassed by his emotions. "You've always been my hero."

His bottom lip trembles and he uses the fingers of his left hand to wipe his eyes. Ali looks at him, full on, for an interminable ten seconds, wanting the fellow to know that he recognizes and honors the personal allegiance the man feels with him. Then my own eyes well up, as do Ali's, and he wipes away his tears with unsteady fingers.

Upon leaving the dealership, Ali is scheduled to have lunch, but he wants to stop at Huntington Beach State Park, where he's been told a group of 450 inner-city kids from Charlotte are being brought on buses to see the ocean for the first time. On the way, he loads up with a new set of Islamic tracts from the reserve he keeps in a second, fat briefcase.

When the limo pulls into the parking lot, the kids haven't arrived. Ali steps from the car and trudges down to the beach. His ever-present dark suit and shiny shoes stand counterpoint to the neon-bright swimwear around him.

The morning fog has burned off and it's nearly ninety degrees in the sun. Ali stands in the shade under a shelter close to the parking lot. After about fifteen minutes, the first bus rolls in. The whole hive of kids, most dressed in swim trunks, some wearing cutoffs and shorts, a couple with ropes tied around their waists, whirl from the vehicle onto the beach, flying off in dozens of trajectories—until a couple of them spot Ali.

They stop, stand and stare, point and elbow each other. Ali closes his hands into fists, puts them beside his head, and makes faces at them, sticking his upper teeth out over his lower lip. When he's certain the kids know him, he drops his arms, opens his hands, and motions them over. A few run to him. He takes the hands of two young girls, one of them about eight years old, the other maybe ten, and walks with them to the bus.

Soon the other buses arrive. Teachers see Ali and race children to get to him. Kids jump up and down in front of Ali and run in circles.

He performs a single magic trick nine times, making a red scarf disappear from his hand, and he signs Muslim pamphlets for all 450 children, the teachers, the bus drivers, and any other beachgoers who want one. "You meant everything to us when we were growing up," one of the drivers says.

A woman in her early forties, wearing a straw hat, green plastic sandals, and a knee-length white T-shirt, runs up to Ali and hugs him big and hard. He leans to kiss her on the cheek; she whispers in his ear; he turns to me. "She's goin' to Loovul," he says, arching his head to make his voice carry farther. As much as anything, that's the connection between us, at least for him—Ali honoring his hometown.

No one seems to remember having come to see the ocean and to swim. Ali mock-boxes with everyone who wants to throw punches with him. He spots a skinny, tough-acting boy of about fourteen, who's wearing long cutoffs, a white T-shirt, and a pair of well-worn Nikes.

Ali points and yells, "You look like Joe Frazuh," contorting his face in feigned anger, and he squares off with the boy.

The kid throws a jab toward Ali's chin, and Ali slips the punch. The boy turns his back and starts to walk away, all the time cutting hard-looking eyes across his shoulder.

Ali takes a long step toward the boy, who gets scared and takes off running. Ali falls in behind. It takes him a couple steps to get going, but soon he's churning his legs so hard that his knees are almost at waist height. They race around a concrete shelter, through a field of grass and a stand of yaupon trees, then out onto the beach. Part of the time, Ali is playing fake-mean; at other moments, he's smiling and chuckling. They run probably two hundred yards down the beach at a dead sprint, this high-strung adolescent in cutoffs and the tired old giant dressed in a custom-tailored suit and shiny leather uppers, which throw small clouds of sand into the air behind him.

About twenty of us go to dinner at an Italian restaurant. Ali and a Muslim who's traveling with him are the only black patrons in the place. As we enter, Ali asks that I be seated across from him. After an expansive meal, he orders a piece of apple pie à la mode.

When the dessert is placed in front of him, he has some trouble with the fork. As he tries to cut bites, a couple forkfuls karom off of the plate and across the tablecloth. He picks up the piece of pie with his fingers and crams it in his mouth. The Muslim seems offended. "*Ali,*" he says, wincing and scowling and shaking his head, glancing at the white faces around him. "Do you *have* to do that?"

Ali lifts the dish and says, "I ain't nothin' but a niggah," then licks the ice cream and the remainder of the pie from the plate.

By nine o'clock, I'm fried. My eyes are droopy, my face feels long and heavy, I can hardly speak. And, of course, I haven't just flown in from China.

It's one o'clock before Ali and I reach the hotel. As I put the key in my lock, I watch him trudge away to his room and think about the grand awkwardness with which he moves. Three hours later, I wake him for the drive to the airport. Ali surely wouldn't be able to go like this for more than a day or two, much less as a way of life, if he didn't regard these trips as his mission.

By six, we've checked in at the gate and he's standing in the middle of the terminal, signing tracts. He doesn't stop until five minutes after the final call for his flight. He surrounds me with his arms, then boards, the last person to get on the plane.

Thirty-one

Two weeks later, I'm en route to Reno when the plane sucks a couple gulls into the aft engine and we land unexpectedly at Pittsburgh airport. As we wait for USAir to find us another plane, I watch a guy on a repair crew crawl up inside the turbines, then I read a magazine, get a cup of frozen yogurt, go for a walk.

After looking around a newsstand and buying a pair of pilot's wings for Isaac, I step outside the terminal, thinking about Ali, thinking he's the only grown person I know who likes airports. I'm reminded of the angels in one of my favorite movies, *Wings of Desire*. Like them, Ali has seen everyone doing everything. None of it matters (the foibles, the scars, the pestilence); all of it resonates (the god in people).

Three crows fly over, one at a time. An elderly couple walk past, hand in hand. The man watches the crows and smiles.

A three-year-old girl with obsidian skin and huge eyes is walking across a parking lot with her mother. She's wearing a pink dress with white lace, a pair of round-toed patent-leather slippers, and her hair is pulled back neatly and is bound by a pink and white bow. "Look, Mama," the daughter says, "there's the moon."

The mother looks up. She hadn't noticed. "Yes, yes, it is," she says, looking pleased.

I walk back into the terminal with a mantra for my trip. *Nothing is mundane; all things vibrate*, I silently repeat as I board the plane.

Thirty-two

The place looks so uninteresting, so forgotten and unimportant, that I drive past without recognizing where I am; we have to turn around and go back.

I park across the road beside the small white mosque and the block-shaped, one-room, knotted cedar cabins in which sparring partners and other entourage members slept. We get out of the rented van, Lyn and Johanna and Isaac and I. We've been in the mountains of West Virginia and western Pennsylvania for a little over a week. We've spent $1,500 of the fifty percent advance for "Zen" on this long-overdue (albeit working) vacation. What with my traveling, money woes, long hours, all the psychic baggage related to the act of writing, and Lyn raising the kids and taking care of the house almost on her own, we can sure use the break.

Before we left home, I called Ali at a Beverly Hills hotel to ask if it'd be okay to visit the Deer Lake training camp.

"My man," he said as he answered the phone. "Where you been? Haven't seen you in a while."

There was the sound of the receiver being dropped. After waiting without success for him to pick it up, I hung up the line.

I tried to call back a few times over the next ten minutes; each time, there was a busy signal. When I finally got through, he picked up on the second ring. "Dropped the phone," he said by way of greeting. His statement was not an apology and, as always, there was no trace of embarrassment. As many calls as he gets, I don't know how he knew the person on the other end of the line would be me.

Now, while the kids climb on the boulders and play with an orange cat, I walk around the cabins, dutifully trying to feel something. Everything is much smaller than I remember, like visiting your old elementary school as an adult. The buckboard is almost exactly where I'd last seen it, right behind the building that once housed the ring. Much of the paint on many of the rocks, expertly applied by old Cash, has been faded by sun and wind or has been washed away by rain and snow. There's one fixture I haven't seen— a granite tombstone that reads ALI'S STAFF, placed to the right of the entrance to the gym by Bundini when camp broke before the Larry Holmes fight in 1980. Seventeen names are inscribed on the monument, including Bingham's, Bundini's, and Angelo Dundee's;

Jimmy Ellis is also there, as well as others I'll never meet, some of whom already have other tombstones in other places.

We take photos of the kids sitting on the rocks and of Isaac giving me a high-five while standing on Sonny Liston. Lyn climbs atop old Jack Johnson; I snap a shot. She and I step across the road and stand beside the van, looking down on the gym and on the Ali living quarters and the kitchen. "Stay here," I say after a minute or two.

I walk back down the hill, still trying to feel something, looking for some sign of the owner, thinking it might work better if I trudge around by myself. I peek in windows at empty walls and bare floors rich with dust, turn rusted doorknobs, steal a piece of bark from the side of the cabin where I had once sparred with Ali. I figure I'll frame it with a picture of the two of us together and hang it on the wall behind my desk. As I pull the crumbling wood from the wall, a droplet of water splashes the back of my hand. I look behind me; a long black cloud is moving in from across the west side of the mountain. A second, tumescent drop hits me dead in the eye.

I jog up the hill to the van, passing the kids as I cross the road. By the time I get the doors unlocked, the air is fragrant with rain; quarter-sized drops drub a syncopated rhythm on the hood. We scramble in and start the engine, barely beating a first-class downpour.

A few miles down the road, headed for Amish country with the windshield wipers on high, I find a public radio station and catch the last few wild bars of a Celtic war song. "That was the Chieftains performing 'The Red Admiral Butterfly,'" a woman announcer says in a husky Scottish brogue, a voice of mist and meadow, forest and dreams.

"Our final song," she says, "was written by blind harper Turlough O'Carolan. Carolan, known as the last great itinerant Irish harper, died on the twenty-fifth of March, 1738, at the age of sixty-eight. He had traveled to Aldeford, to the home of his lifetime patron and sponsor. When he arrived at the house, he called for his harp, wrote and played 'Carolan's Farewell to Music.' He then retired to bed, where he died."

As the centuries-old melody wafts from the speakers, I ask Lyn what she thought of the old Ali haunt. "It was all right," she says, "but I didn't feel any of his greatness there."

She sounds surprised and a bit disappointed. I tell her that it makes sense that she wouldn't; it simply confirms what Ali says just about every time I've been with him.

"All the things I've done, all the praise, all the fame, don't none of it mean nothin'. It's all only dust."

Thirty-three

The fee I'm paid by the men's monthly allows me to work on "Zen" in a fairly unpressured way, without having to shill for additional assignments to meet the bills week to week, a privilege I've not previously been able to enjoy.

From the first day of writing, the story seems to step from the shadows to walk with me. When I take a breath, I feel "Zen" in my bones. Telling this story seems as necessary as are those bones for movement.

When I deliver the piece in late August, I'm ecstatic. I believe that this is the very story that will make my career.

My editor calls quickly, agreeing with me. "It may be the best writing ever about Ali," he says. "We're going to get a lot of attention for this. Can we get him to sit for a portrait?"

What to tell the guy? I haven't asked anything of Ali since that first rejection. And mostly not because of his reaction. Ali knows me better now and understands that I write for a living. He and Lonnie both like what I've written. But I don't like to ask anything of him. I haven't taken his picture, don't take pictures with him, don't ask him to stand up and pose, to do anything other than what he is doing, who he is being.

So I guess I startle myself when I offer to set up a photo shoot. "I'll give him a call and let you know what he says," I tell my editor.

The second week of September, it has turned cold in Michigan, which surprises me. When I get to the farm, I'm wearing shorts and a T-shirt that features a photo of Ali spanking Floyd Patterson in their first bout. There's sometimes a price to pay for not watching television or reading newspapers. This time the toll is the goose bumps on my arms and legs.

As I step from the car, the new groundskeeper, a bespectacled fellow who reminds me of an old sea captain, sees the raised hairs on my legs and goes out to the gym, returning with a pair of blue warm-ups I've often seen Ali wearing. "Here, put these on," he says, handing me the pants.

Floyd's no longer at the farm. Although I wonder where he's gone, there's no use asking Ali. I doubt that he would remember. People come into, and go from, Ali's life all the time. I suppose that I'll probably do so, too.

The magazine has sent a photographer from Manhattan, a guy I like a lot, who has a gentle demeanor and a kind of mystery about him, as well as a plenty wonderful name—Len Irish. Len asks me to take off my shirt and go stand at the fence beside the barn. He takes a shot of me wearing Ali's britches pulled all the way up to my nipples.

Inside, I introduce Len to Lonnie, then to Ali, who is at his desk. Ali stands when he sees us. Although Len has worked with dozens of celebrities, he visibly shakes when he reaches for Ali's hand.

"Davy," Ali says, "my man." It's the first time he has known my name.

Ali asks what I'm working on other than the story about him. I tell him that I'd like to ride on the space shuttle and write a book about the experience. "I'll be the Greatest Writing Astronaut of All Times," I say in my Ali voice, which has improved from spending so much time with the Man himself. And I'm interested in hanging out with and writing about Jimmy Carter, I tell him.

"He's smart," says Ali. "Buildin' houses for poor people. Doin' it with his own hands. I got all the money I need. Want to give every penny I make from now on to charities, to help people. Don't matter if I make forty-three million. Gonna give it all away."

Len excuses himself to go outside and set up for our portrait. I stay behind, telling Ali about "Zen" and how much I like the story. "When I was young, I always knew there'd be somebody like you," he says. "Always knew you'd come along."

"You mean that, don't you?" I say. "You did know, didn't you?"

He nods.

"How did you know?" I ask.

He can't say.

But maybe I can. Or at least I can propose a theory. Ali's proclamation isn't founded simply in the freedom of an illusion that seems borne out by facts. Nor is it so much arrogance as it is a sure sense of his own personal destiny. Perhaps he was born to live out a mythology, to reveal for us, among other things, the dharma of self-importance. And maybe I'm the vehicle that relays this myth. Or maybe the mythology is only my own. Either way, one of its morals is that we cannot invent ourselves, that the twentieth-century religion of self-actualization is a current illusion.

"I didn't make myself and you didn't make yourself," Ali has often told me. "All the things people praise me for, I didn't do those myself. We don't choose to draw air into our own lungs. We don't decide who we are or where we're born."

On this visit, as on every other before or since, the one predictable thing about Ali is that the *I am* of him sloshes out of the pails we attempt to carry him in. For more than thirty years, Ali has caused us to question our concepts of reality. As Len sets up his first shot, at a place near the pool where he likes the quality of light and the view of trees near the horizon, Ali opens a storage room, pulling out flotation rings and a half-inflated plastic float, which he plops into the deepest water. Watching me, Ali, who can't swim a lick, convincingly pretends that he's going to walk off of the edge and into nine feet of water.

Ali's facial features have much of the muscular rigidity, the "mask," that is associated with Parkinsonism. Despite this, when Len is ready, Ali allows Len to take shot after tight shot of his face on roll after roll of film. An hour later, as we ready ourselves to go back in the house, knowing that Len can't possibly get a picture with the kind of equipment he has brought and the way in which he has it set up, Ali opens the door to the garage and rides out on a neon-yellow bicycle, which he tools once around the driveway as Len rolls his eyes over the missed shot. Ali then puts the bike away and asks if I'd like to go for a ride in the Rolls, which he proceeds to drive bouncingly through the fields as if it were a plow.

As we step from the car with me still wearing Ali's pants and the T-shirt with his image on the back, Len has finally removed his camera from its tripod and has attached a lens he can use for candid action. As Len shoots away, Ali squares off with me and we toss a few punches at one another. "I could be your son," I say, "if I was black."

Inside the house, as Ali and I wait for Len to set up a second portrait near the pond, Ali listens to a Little Richard cassette with a tinny, vibrating jam box pressed all the way up against his right cheek, though he is standing less than ten feet away from a $2,000 sound system. As "Tutti-Frutti" is being drilled into his inner ear, with his eyes closed Ali points at the speaker, shouting "The King, the King," speaking of the singer and not of himself. Len comes in to say that he's ready. Ali motions for him to sit at the kitchen table, where Ali proceeds to serve us vanilla ice cream honorifically, with high sacrament, studying Len's face and mine to see if we properly appreciate his gift, which is not so much the ice cream as it is his act of giving. Yet, of the thirty or so meals I've taken with Ali and/or have seen him eat, vanilla ice cream has been served with probably twenty-five of them.

Outside, Ali takes a seat on a bar stool that Len has set up on the high ground above the pond. Ali's eyes are inordinately sensitive to light; for this reason, he often wears sunglasses in public. Now, with wind and sun in direct contact with his face, he blinks rapidly, almost uncontrollably. "Don't need this shit no more," he says to me of the photo session. "Doin' this as a favor for you."

Other than Howard's photos, this has been the first group of portraits Ali has sat for in years. I tell Len that we've gotten enough, that we have all of the pictures we need. "Man, this makes me feel so bad," I tell the Champ. "I'm sorry I asked you to do this."

He turns his head, looking at me, gets up from the stool, and with me beside him, starts back toward the house. He drops his long arm across my shoulders and tells me absolutely the worst joke I have ever heard. "A chicken ain't nothin' but a bird," he says. "A white man ain't nothin' but a turd. And a niggah . . . ain't nothin'."

Awful as it is, I can't help but laugh.

That evening, Len and I take Ali and Lonnie to dinner in St. Joseph. As we wait for our meal and Ali sleeps and signs autographs for waiters, kitchen staff, and customers, I mention to Lonnie that Ali seems pleased with the big-screen TV a local merchant gave him. "When he's home," she says, "he watches news stations hour after hour. About the only thing that makes him turn it off is when he wants to play with his new pet."

"I didn't think you had pets," I say. "I didn't think he cared anything about dogs and cats."

"This is a big animal. Didn't you see it out in the pasture? Why don't you mention it in your story? This fan in Africa gave him a rhinoceros."

"Gave him a what?"

"A rhinoceros. As big a fan as you are, Davy, you must've heard about Muhammad's rhino."

"No, no, tell me about it," I say.

She laughs right out loud and turns away, blushing. "April Fools'," says the wife of the Greatest Jokester of All Times.

Thirty-four

I tell you, you just can't count on anything when you're doing magazine work.

"Davis, I need to apologize," says the first world-class editor with whom I would've had the opportunity to work. "I'm not going to be editing your piece. We're in a time crunch for this first issue and I have to pull it all together. We've just hired a senior editor and he'll work with you. I'll ask him to call you later today."

"I'm not as impressed with this piece as John is," says the assignment editor. "It needs some harder reporting. I want you to talk with Ali's attorneys, his accountants, his doctors. What's the situation with his health and his finances? That's what people want to know. I've read your story three times and I still don't know what the point is."

Oh, no. Not now. Not this story, I think. This one's just too important to me. "I can't do that," I say. "It's not our business to speak with his doctors, accountants, et cetera."

From his cubicle six hundred miles away, I see this guy put his hand over his eyes and shake his head. He doesn't know what to make of me any more than he does of "Zen."

"Besides, you're trying to put art in a box," I say.

He laughs at me without taking his mouth away from the receiver. "What's the point?" he repeats, flat, almost tough.

"There is no point," I say.

I wait for him to reply. He doesn't. I go on. "Nothing can *define* Ali," I tell him. "Or us."

"Look, you're a good writer," he says soothingly, "but I'm not satisfied with this piece. We're going to have to do a rewrite."

Man, I can't believe this, I just can't believe it. Trying to act calm, wanting to be a professional, I say, "I'll call tomorrow and let you know what I can do."

What's the point?

The nonpoint of art is this: It's a rhythm that makes you want to dance. It's a dance that helps you feel. It's a shelter to keep you out of the wind that cracks bones.

From the beginning, I guess I've suspected that someone would eventually expect me to *report* about Ali. I'm just not going to do it.

This whole situation makes me feel unclean. And

it's weird that Ali warned me about this kind of thing when I asked him if he'd be photographed for "My Dinner." Although it was part of his group-speak, a canned reaction, it's still pretty remarkable.

What is identity? Is there such a thing? Why even try for factual accuracy? Resonance affects us more deeply than does meaning. What we feel is richer than are "facts." The journalistic method reduces reality to that which seems understandable. It caters to the kind of small-smart mind that thinks we can know, accepts that we can know, needs a point. At least that's my way of seeing it.

Whenever I've heard people say who Ali is (including me), they've been less than right. Ali recognizes this and often takes pleasure from it.

Compartmentalizing. One of the most important things I've learned from Ali is that we're incorrect when we say who anyone is, or isn't. Everyone's life is rounder and more complex than we take it to be. The only time we can safely box someone (anyone!) is when he's dead and we plant him in the ground or place his ashes on our mantels.

Boxing, framing, naming may be the very cause of disturbing that in which I've often found the greatest pleasure, the most solace: the natural world, that place which, until recently, seemed sacrosanct, irreducible; if not exempt from the knife, the slicing of the pie, the reductionism of Western let's-make-everything-better science, the discounting of modernity (of which journalism is a part), then damned close to it.

Storytelling seems a more round and honest (and less harmful) way of being in the world than "straight" journalism. I'm not after the "facts" about Ali, or anyone else. What I seek is this: to find the story that is the richest, the most compelling, the most *truthful*, tale that I can tell. Truthful in what I hope to be the largest way. I can't pretend to know Ali's life. What I know is my story—not even my own life, but the story I tell about it, as the story develops, *as I write it*. In this very moment. Which isn't the same as my memories of what happened. A good writer can always, will always, imagine a different, a "better," *more fitting*, detail than that which memory supplies. And, as the story is written, it takes on its own life, a shimmering, quivering "dream" of an existence that, in some ways, is more real than the things experienced in day-to-day, "wakeful" life. The shining details provided by my writer's imagination (the very imagination that Ali helped to cultivate in me) are always more real than confirmable phenomena, than the "facts."

Yet, there's no way around it—I need the money. And this is far and away the best and biggest magazine I've had the opportunity to be published in.

Lyn calls from work, upset. A friend who had taken a year off from her job to be with her husband—he was only forty, in perfect health, a runner, ate well, looked terrific, just had a treadmill, which came up perfect—the fellow died during the night.

How are we to react to this? How are we to live?

People on air crashes: Does anyone feel it coming? How are we to know what to do?

I don't know. And I'm not going to know. None of

us is going to know. Every way we deal with it must be exactly the right way.

"Just go for a walk in the woods," I say to Lyn. "Stare at the sun through leaves. I don't know what else to do, what else there is."

As we hang up, I recognize that I'm playing a CD of Japanese melodies called *Sakura*. Sakura: "Cherry Blossoms"—here now and gone so very quickly, those ancient symbols of impermanence.

I walk to the open front door, watch the stark gold light of ozone-depleted autumn on the black-barked maple in the front yard. Beside the door, the Fed Ex guy has left a package of Ali videocassettes from a fan of my stories who lives in New Jersey. When I pop a tape in the VCR, I'm struck once again by Ali's innocence: "See my nose, look at my face," he says in a 1972 black and white interview for Irish television. "Most fighters have a nose like that (squashes his with his index finger), have ears like this (pulls them away from his head). I'm pretty! And I'm the onliest fighter that can talk."

Sure, I wish that Ali would live for a thousand years. Yet, I recognize that he already has: He's seen and done and *been* so much. The way Ali lives now, most every day, of every year, is at least as remarkable as what he did with the body of a young god. I can't imagine anyone whose time on this planet—including through his illness, maybe *especially* through his illness—has been more life-affirming than that of Muhammad Ali.

Thirty-five

I rewrite the piece. After all, it's not the magazine I have a problem with. Just this fast-food-style editor whose patty is over-formed and undercooked. And I don't give him what he wants, or expects. He gets a little "Zen" (because it's my art) and a little of what Muhammad and Lonnie would like (details of Ali's kindness, his role as world emissary). It's a perfectly harmless, "informative" article.

The editor is relatively pleased, I get my check, and "Zen" remains my child.

As Len Irish develops photos to be run with the article, he calls to let me know how happy he is with the head shot. "He looks like the Mona Lisa," Len says. "Timeless, satisfied, spiritual.

"You know, Ali was in town last week," he tells me. "This is going to sound silly, but I kept expecting him to give me a call. I spent just a few hours with him and he makes you feel so close to him you think he's your friend. I was kind of disappointed he didn't call."

When *Men's Journal* publishes my piece in its first issue, Muhammad leaves a message on my answering machine: "This is the Greatest Niggah of All Times," he says. Lonnie hates it when he does this stuff. "Give me a call. Here's the number."

He hands the phone to Howard, who leaves the number of a hotel in Shanghai. When I next catch up with Ali, when he gets back to the States, he tells me how much he enjoyed the story, which he probably wouldn't have done with "Zen."

I get lucky with "Zen," but not in the United States, at least at first. I sell the story to the British edition of *Esquire*, where I'm treated kindly and where I'll soon write other pieces. And when every magazine editor that I contact in the States tells me the same old crap I'm used to hearing from them, I sell "Zen" as the cover piece for newspaper magazines all over the United States, as well as in Ireland and Brazil. I get hundreds of letters from folks around the country, and "Zen" is nominated for a Pulitzer Prize by my editor at the Miami *Herald*. It also inspires an hour-long ESPN documentary about the current Ali. All of which puts me well on my way to making it as a writer.

Thirty-six

Serendipity. For months, the word has again been on my tongue. On Wednesday, February 5, I pack the Volvo with two suitcases. At ten A.M., I pick Isaac up at school and we leave Winston-Salem, bound for Berrien Springs.

No one knows we're coming. I wanted to call the farm to see if it was okay for us to visit, but Lonnie changes numbers more often than nuclear weapons facilities switch security codes, and I don't have a current number. But although Ali has been traveling almost constantly, I'm (again) confident that if we drive up now, we'll be able to get with him. I have no reason to believe otherwise: Things have always worked out when it comes to connecting with Ali.

Isaac and I make it to the farm around dusk on Thursday. It's only three weeks after the Champ's

fiftieth birthday, and my fortieth. The wrought-iron
gates are locked and the big MUHAMMAD ALI FARMS
sign has been removed. When Ali is home, I've never
seen the gates closed.

A light snow is falling; behind the dark metal bars,
it sparkles on Ali's driveway. Isaac is more excited by
the snow than about the opportunity of meeting Ali.
We seldom see the white stuff in Winston anymore.
When I was a kid, we'd get several inches a couple
times a year.

I step carefully from the car and push the small red
button on the shining stainless intercom. To our
right, a horse the color of hot chocolate is standing at
a fence, shaking snow from its mane.

Lonnie's brother Mike answers on the fifth ring.
After I explain who I am and what I want, he says,
"They're not here. They haven't been home since
Christmas and I don't expect them for two to three
weeks."

I tell Mike I have videocassette copies of a few of
Muhammad's fights and interviews that I'd promised
to mail to Lonnie. "Bring them on down," he says.
"I'll open the gate."

Mike opens the door to the kitchen, carrying a
small cardboard box full of white paper packets.
"Time to get the seeds ready for planting," he says.
The past two years, he tells us, he's been tending an
acre of vegetables he's grown for the family's use, as
well as for the homeless of nearby Benton Harbor.

I hand Mike the videotapes and copies of newspaper pieces I'd written for the Champ's fiftieth. As

Isaac and I turn to leave for our long drive home, the phone rings. Mike answers it in the adjoining den.

While Mike is out of the room, I tell Isaac, "I'm sorry you didn't get to meet Ali, but we've had a good time staying in hotels and we'll have a good time on the way home."

Just then, Mike comes back into the kitchen. "Man, you're lucky," he says. "That was Lonnie. They'll get in late tonight. She said for you to come by first thing tomorrow."

Lonnie opens the back door, carrying ten-month-old Asaad, whose hair is in a top-knot, almost Japanese style. Asaad is large for his age. He's been walking since he was six months and Lonnie tells me he weighs over thirty pounds. Asaad sees Isaac and struggles to get down. Isaac, who's typically uncomfortable around babies, is surprisingly attracted to Asaad: He playfully pulls on the toddler's foot and tweaks his stomach.

"Muhammad will want to meet you," I tell him. "Then you can play."

I've driven Isaac a thousand miles for this next moment, and I'm anxious to see it.

Isaac and I step through the kitchen and into the family room. To our right, in the far corner, Ali is sitting at his desk, signing pamphlets. Three full, open suitcases are at his feet. He's barefoot and not wearing a shirt. He's nearly as round as old Bodhidharma himself.

Ali looks at me and nods, almost invisibly, then

reaches his arms out to my son, who moves slowly, reverentially, forward. Ali's arms encircle him. Isaac has never had a strange man hug him like this, but I can tell by his expression that with Ali he doesn't mind. Indeed, he is flattered: He's smiling the proudest, nicest, most self-assured smile I've seen on his features.

"You'll remember this when you're an old, old man," Ali says, both to me and to my son.

As he places Isaac on his knee, Ali nods toward me again. He wants to be certain I don't feel slighted. "Happy birthday, Champ," I say.

When Isaac hops down, Ali pulls a flannel shirt and a pair of white athletic socks from a suitcase, tugs them on, slips into a pair of black dress shoes. He turns to Isaac, who's playing with one of Asaad's toy cars. "Stay here," Ali says with respectful authority. "We'll be back." He waves for me to follow.

We go outside, stepping across the driveway to the garage. The day glows phosphorescently; snow is coming down in chunks the size of an infant's hands. We enter the garage through a side door and climb a set of stairs. At the top, we pass a big, elegant desk, then turn right and walk down a short hallway. He pulls open a door. An otherwise empty space, about the size of a master bedroom, is piled floor to ceiling with boxes and envelopes and packages. "This is the mail I don't have time to open," he says.

"How long did it take to get this much?" I ask.

"About six months."

I grab the two pieces closest to my foot. The top

one is covered with brightly colored stamps. "From Indonesia," the experienced traveler says.

I feel a videocassette inside. The other is a thick letter on onionskin paper; the return address is in Kansas.

"Yesterday I was in Washington, at the Pentagon. I'm always somewhere. Want you to help me. Feel bad not bein' able to write everybody."

This is in no way an overstatement. Nearly every day, when he's home, Ali invests three to four hours in opening letters and writing replies. He seems to feel it's part of his mission to contact every person on the planet.

"Want to get a 900 number, where people can call and get a message, where I can talk with them. You're my man. Want you to find out how to do it."

We walk back to his office. He points to a phone on the desk. "Can you call from here?" he says. "Find out somethin'."

He motions me into his intricately carved chair. "If I can just get my voice straightened out," he continues, easing onto a smaller chair on the opposite side of the desk, "I want to do this."

"If you want, I'll help," I say. But there's something I'd like to know.

"At the Frazier dinner, when you got up to speak, you talked for probably ten minutes. You didn't slur or stammer, your volume was fine, you were funny, your timing was good."

It's true. He was terrific. And I've seen the same thing happen on several occasions over the past years, always when there are no TV cameras on him. "How do you do that?" I ask.

He doesn't tell me. I doubt he knows. Instead, he falls into his old prefight voice.

"This is Muhammad Ali, the Greatest of All Times. I did what I set out to do. Whupped Sonny Liston, whupped Joe Frazier, George Foreman, whupped the United States draft board."

After thirty seconds or so, he stops and rubs his left hand across his face in the way I do when I've just woken from a night's sleep. "See wh-wh-what you can find out," he asks. His voice gurgles like the river behind his property.

I make calls and get basic information about 900 numbers. As we leave the garage, headed for the house, Lonnie, Asaad, and Isaac meet us halfway.

"Saadie wanted to go with you, Muhammad," Lonnie says. She hands the child to her husband and looks at his slick-soled shoes. "Don't you dare drop that baby," she says. Her tone is wifely, concerned, but not patronizing. She turns and goes back to the house.

With Ali and Asaad in the lead, we trudge around the driveway. Soon, Ali's son decides he wants down. Ali lowers him to the ground, holding his left hand, and tries to get him to walk. Asaad turns to look at Isaac; he intends to play. I ask Isaac to take Asaad's right hand so he'll go with his daddy. My boy does so in a way that replicates Ali's gentleness. I stay a few feet behind, watching the three of them shuffle along at a ten-month-old's pace. For many minutes, Ali,

Asaad, and Isaac plod back and forth in a chain through the snow. The only sounds are those of wind in bare rattling branches of trees and of Ali's scuffling feet and, in the distance, of water tumbling over rocks. Just before we go back inside, I reach to brush melting snow from the children's hair and shoulders, and from Ali's.

Lonnie and Asaad leave for the grocery store. Ali, Isaac, and I park ourselves on the sofa and put on a videotape of the Champ's fight with Chuck Wepner. There's no commentary on this version. On the huge stereo TV, you hear Bundini yelling from the corner, Ali talking to Wepner, the punches as they connect, and Ali's feet as he springs around the canvas. It's almost the experience of attending the fight live. Although I'm aware that Ali is playing the Wepner bout for my entertainment, the old narcissist becomes immediately riveted by his own image. Watching him silently concentrate on the first three rounds, he seems ageless. That is, his youth, middle years, and old age are all on his features. As he intently (religiously?) studies his own history on the screen, his hands and head stop trembling. I ask what he's thinking about.

"I forget how good I was, what I used to could do," he says.

During the fourth round, the phone rings. Ali answers and listens for a moment. "You don't have no business callin' here, disturbin' my peace," he says.

"I'm retired. Want to be left alone. Don't care nothin' 'bout boxin'."

He cups his hand over the phone and looks slyly at me. "Famous boxin' promoter," he says. Then into the phone: "You say it's important because it's important to you. It don't mean nothin' to me. Boxin's dyin'. I always said it'd die when I left. Just look at it—there's Tyson. But he's no Muhammad Ali, no kind of real hero. I ain't goin' to your fights. I'm aware of my condition—all those people around, me shakin', press writin' about how pitiful I am. Don't need it. Don't call here no more, niggah."

While he's talking, I notice a letter on the coffee table and see that it's from Oliver Stone. Ali spots me reading and hangs up the phone without saying anything else to the caller.

He points at the letter. "Wants to give me about three million dollars to sign my life away. Don't care nothin' 'bout the money. It don't mean nothin' to me. Wouldn't mind a movie bein' made, if it was a good movie, about what's important. He'd want to make it sensational—that ain't my way no more."

Although I'm sure my doubts about Stone's ability to make a solid Ali film are somewhat different from Ali's own concerns, it hardly seems possible that elephant-fisted Ollie would subtly replicate even the most basic events of Ali's huge, seemingly contradictory life, much less have any real sense of the complexities of his spirituality.

"I'd hate to see you made into some kind of cartoon," I tell him.

"I'm fifty years old now," he says. "That doesn't seem possible. When they gowna leave me alone, when is all this gowna stop? I wanta take two years off, quit all this travelin'. Stay home with my wife and son."

I've heard him say this kind of thing before, but within fifteen minutes have had him ask to go to a shopping mall, where he'll sit and sign autographs for two to three hours at a time.

I get ready to tell him the obvious—that he'll never be left alone and he wouldn't like it if he were—but then Lonnie and Asaad come in from the store and I don't say anything. She steps into the den with a pack of Bubblicious bubblegum, which she hands to Isaac. Asaad is tagging along, wanting a piece for himself. "You're too young, Saadie," she says.

Ali widens his eyes. "How about me?" he asks.

To me she says, "Muhammad can't keep gum out of his mouth. Go look under his desk."

I get up from the sofa, walk across the room, lean low, take a peek. Sure enough, there are dozens of fat pink wads all rammed up under the Great Man's formal mahogany desk.

I look across at him and begin to laugh; he's staring at me with a guilty grin that's in no way an affectation. "I know why you think it's funny," he says. "You have gum underneath your desk, too."

For lunch, Lonnie broils fat turkey burgers for Ali and me and makes a cheese sandwich for Isaac. She brings the food on metal lunch trays. "Here, Punkin," she says as she places Ali's tray in his lap.

Yes! "Punkin."

How could any nickname be more perfect? His Southernness, the playfulness, the association with warmth and comfort, his squnchability, his roundness. Even Ali's skin is pumpkin-colored.

On the same plate as his burger, Muhammad has three pills he's supposed to take every day (but which he almost never does—unless Lonnie sees to it): a red one, a blue one, and an orange one. And a piece of bubblegum.

Isaac and I stay at the farm for two days. Ali plays with my son hour upon hour, doing magic tricks, scaring and enchanting him with horror stories ("I'm Frankenstein," says the King of All Children. "I'm gowna eat you up"), chasing him around the house, hiding behind furniture, jumping out to tickle him. "When I was thirty," Ali confides, "I used to wonder when I was gowna quit playin'. Used to sorta worry about it. Now I know I'm never gowna quit." When he isn't entertaining Isaac or talking with me, he's often asleep and snoring.

As we leave for our long drive home, he walks us to the car. As always, he hugs me, and I recognize that his touch goes through the me, past the me, to the everyone, to the everywhere. I turn the key in the ignition. He closes our doors.

It's still snowing, yet surprisingly, there's little accumulation. Just enough to make the asphalt slippery. Like Lonnie, I'm concerned that Muhammad might fall. There's a video camera in the backseat. When

I'm certain that Ali's balance is okay, I grab it and push the power button.

Ali sees the camera and opens Isaac's door, snatching up my son. For a moment, as he holds Isaac for the camera, there's paramount seriousness about Ali, a purposeful profundity in the eyes: He wants me (and, through the electronic lens, wants each of us) to know that the care he is giving my son (and that he'll afford anyone's child) is of the angels. Then he blinks and, as he pulls my son higher, holding him at face level, the moment has passed.

"This is the next champion," Ali says, tugging language up from the labyrinth. "This man will win the crown in 2020. Look at the face. 2020. Just think about it: I will be the manager. I'll be ninety-three. And we will be the greatest of *that* day, the greatest of *that* time."

Ali places my laughing son back in his seat and points at the lens. "Watch my feet," he says in the old voice, the thick one, the one of smoke and dreams. He turns his back and takes about ten shuffling steps. There's a moment when the car engine stops, the wind doesn't move, the air is not cold.

Looking over his left shoulder, Ali raises his arms perpendicular to his sides. And although I've seen this illusion many, many times, I'm still impressed as the most famous man in the world seemingly rises from the earth once more.

"This is Muhammad Ali in Berrien Springs, Michigan," he says. "Ain't nobody else like me. Joe Louis, Ray Robinson, they just boxers. I'm the biggest thing that ever happened in sports. I ain't boastin'; it's just the way it is. From Adam until now, I am the greatest in the recorded history of mankind," he says to the camera, and to the world.

As we pull out of the driveway, Isaac is sitting all the way in the back of the car, staring out the rear window. I ask my son if he is crying. He nods yes. I ask why. "He's so cool, I didn't think anybody could be that cool. I just wish he wasn't sick."

I tell him that it's all right. And I honestly think that it is. Even more than all right, Ali's life has been exactly what it was intended to be. With Ali, I have traveled through great beauty to some measure of understanding; I have learned about flow and about mortality. We are water and old stars. You can't ask for more than that.

Thirty-seven

The following week, I go to Isaac's school to talk with his classmates about our visit to the farm. I ask the first-graders how many of them have heard of Muhammad Ali. It has been nearly thirty years since that moonless night in Miami when he befuddled Sonny Liston; almost twenty since he turned George Foreman inside out and won back the heavyweight title in Zaire—then two hours later the monsoons set in; almost as long since the "Thrilla in Manila," when he thoroughly whupped Joe Frazier in 115-degree heat. All twenty-three six-year-olds raise their hands.

After I speak for a few minutes and answer questions, Isaac reads an Ali story he has written. We play a videocassette that includes highlights from the Champ's career, as well as the levitation scene we'd taped at the farm. At the end of class, kids erupt into the hallway shouting, "Float like a butterfly, sting like a bee" and "I'm a *baadd* man." Everybody, including the girls, throws punches at everybody else. The teachers look shocked. I'm sure I won't be invited back anytime soon.

For days thereafter, my son tells me, he reminds his classmates that they have seen a man named Muhammad Ali who can actually fly.